Corporate Insolvency

Cavendish
Publishing
Limited

London • Sydney • Portland, Oregon

This book is supported by a Companion Website, created to keep titles in the *Pocket Lawyer* **series up to date and to provide enhanced resources for readers.**

Key features include:

◆ forms and letters, in a ready-to-use Word format
   Access all the material you need at the click of a button

◆ updates on key developments
   Your book won't become out of date

◆ links to useful websites
   No more fruitless internet searches

www.cavendishpublishing.com/pocketlawyer

Corporate Insolvency

Andrew McTear, Chris Williams,
Frank Brumby & Rosy Border

Cavendish
Publishing
Limited

London • Sydney • Portland, Oregon

First published in Great Britain 2004 by
Cavendish Publishing Limited, The Glass House,
Wharton Street, London WC1X 9PX, United Kingdom
Telephone: + 44 (0)20 7278 8000   Facsimile: + 44 (0)20 7278 8080
Email: info@cavendishpublishing.com
Website: www.cavendishpublishing.com

Published in the United States by Cavendish Publishing
c/o International Specialized Book Services,
5824 NE Hassalo Street, Portland,
Oregon 97213-3644, USA

Published in Australia by Cavendish Publishing (Australia) Pty Ltd
45 Beach Street, Coogee, NSW 2034, Australia
Email: info@cavendishpublishing.com.au
Website: www.cavendishpublishing.com.au

British Library Cataloguing in Publication Data
McTear, Andrew
Corporate Insolvency – 2nd ed – (Pocket lawyer)
1 Collection laws – England 2 Collection laws – Wales
I Title II Border, Rosy

Library of Congress Cataloguing in Publication Data
Data available

ISBN 1-85941-925-9

3 5 7 9 10 8 6 4 2

Printed and bound in Great Britain

Contents

Disclaimer

This book puts *you* in control. This is an excellent thing, but it also makes *you* responsible for using it properly. Few washing machine manufacturers will honour their guarantee if you don't follow their 'instructions for use'. In the same way, we are unable to accept liability for any loss arising from mistakes or misunderstandings on your part. So please take time to read this book carefully.

Although this book points you in the right direction, reading one small book will not make you an expert, and it can certainly never replace the need to take professional advice. This book is not a definitive statement of the law, although we believe it to be accurate as at April 2004.

The authors and publisher cannot accept liability for any advice or material that becomes obsolete due to changes in the law after the publication date, although every effort will be made to show any such changes on the companion website.

About the authors

Andrew McTear and **Chris Williams** are Chartered Accountants, practising Licensed Insolvency Practitioners and partners in East Anglian-based business rescue and insolvency specialists McTear Williams & Wood. They work closely with **Frank Brumby**, who is a Licensed Insolvency Practitioner and a partner at Leathes Prior solicitors. All three work closely with individuals and directors of companies in financial difficulty, or their advisors, and they see at first hand the issues that most affect directors of under-performing companies on a daily basis.

Rosy Border, co-author of this title and series editor of the *Pocket Lawyer* series, has worked in publishing, lecturing, journalism and the law. A prolific author and adapter, she stopped counting after 150 titles. She enjoys DIY, entertaining and retail therapy in French markets.

Acknowledgments

A glance at the 'Useful contacts' section will show the many individuals and organisations we consulted while compiling this book. Thank you, everyone.

Frank, Andrew and Chris would particularly like to thank David Wood of McTear Williams & Wood and Sue Sutton of Leathes Prior Solicitors, who provided invaluable suggestions, and long suffering secretaries, Julie and Linda, for their support. Rosy owes a debt of gratitude to her husband, John Rabson, for IT support and coffee.

CORPORATE INSOLVENCY

Welcome

Welcome to *Pocket Lawyer*. Let's face it – the law is a maze. Without a map you are likely to get lost. This book is your map through the part of the maze that deals with under-performing companies and their directors. It is a big subject, but this book outlines everything the experts would tell you if only they had the time and you had the money to pay them.

If you follow our advice you should be able to:

o   recognise when you are in financial difficulty;
o   know what your main options are;
o   make informed choices;
o   having made those choices, understand what the other actors in the drama are likely to do and what happens next;
o   know when you are out of your depth and need to seek professional advice.

We put *you* in control

This book empowers you. This is a good thing, but control carries responsibility as well as power, so please use this book properly. Read it with care. We have left wide margins for you to make notes. Take your time – do not skip anything:

o   everything is there for a purpose;
o   if anything were unimportant, we would have left it out.

Think of yourself as a driver using a road map. The map tells you the route, but it is up to you to drive carefully along it.

As with any legal matter, your own common sense will often tell you when you are out of your depth and need expert help. We warn you when you are in danger of getting lost and need to take professional advice. We will alert you to:

o   common traps for the unwary;
o   situations when you are in danger of getting out of your depth and need to take professional advice.

Watch out for the hazard sign.

Sometimes we stop to empower you to do something. Look out for this sign.

Sometimes we pause to explain something: the origin of a word, perhaps, or why a particular piece of legislation was passed. You do not need to know these things to make use of this book, but we hope you find them interesting.

Clear English rules OK

Client to solicitor who has just drafted a contract for him: 'This *can't* be legal – I can understand it!'

Our style is WYSIWYG – what you see is what you get.

Some legal documents have traditionally been written in archaic language, often known as 'law-speak'. This term also extends to the practice of using the names of legal cases as shorthand for legal concepts. This wording has stood the test of time – often several centuries – and has been hallowed by the courts. Some of the words used sound just like everyday language, but beware – it is a kind of specialist shorthand. When we *do* need to use technical language, we offer clear explanations in 'Buzzwords', p xiii. These words appear in the text in **bold** so that you can check their meaning.

A note about Scotland and Northern Ireland

The regime for corporate insolvencies in Scotland and Northern Ireland is very similar to England and Wales. While some of the forms and detailed procedures are different, the advice in this book does, in the main, apply.

A note on gender

This book is unisex. Where possible, we use the generic *they/them* rather than *he/she/him/her*, etc.

Click onto the website

www.cavendishpublishing.com/pocketlawyer

What this book can do for you

This book:

o   provides general information. Insolvency is a big subject and key decisions often require finely balanced judgments. This book puts these into context, but it is not a substitute for talking the situation through with a valued friend *or taking professional advice;*

o   tells you the buzzwords which are important in this section of the law and what they mean;

o   answers some of the most frequently asked questions on the subject;

o   is supported by a regularly updated website.

What this book can't do for you

This book cannot be a textbook (the leading textbook on corporate insolvencies alone would make four very good doorstops). Its job is to point you in the right direction and put what is likely to happen in context, not to teach you the ins and outs of insolvency law. We aim for you to be streetwise rather than academic.

Can you DIY?

- Corporate insolvency is not a self-help regime, but this book aims to explain the various procedures. It will enable you to understand and interact with the Insolvency Practitioner.
- On the other hand, turnaround *can* be a self-help exercise and the book shows you what to consider when under financial pressure.

Insolvency is not a DIY subject (see above). Most procedures require the involvement of an **Insolvency Practitioner** (see 'Buzzwords') and require their consent to act as such. It follows that, in this field, one of your most important decisions is your choice of Insolvency Practitioner. Every industry has its bad eggs, so it is often best to go with a personal recommendation, perhaps from your accountant or someone who has been through the mill themselves.

There is bound to be a reputable Insolvency Practitioner near you. There really is no need to allow yourself to be referred to a practitioner on the other side of the country by a debt advisor acting as a middle man – you may have received numerous letters from these people already if you have a county court judgment reported against you.

Buzzwords

As we said, many trades and professions use special words in the course of their work, or use ordinary words in a different way from those outside their own group. Eavesdrop on any gathering of doctors, lawyers, plumbers or motor mechanics and you'll see what we mean. The world of insolvency is no exception. Here are some expressions you will find helpful. When a buzzword crops up in the main text of the book, we mark it in **bold**.

administration – the aim of administration is to allow the company to be rehabilitated or reorganised if this is achievable or, if not, to ensure the most profitable realisation of the company's *assets*. The directors can put a company directly into administration by *filing* the necessary papers in court. Alternatively, the directors, shareholders or a *creditor* can make an application to the court for an *administration order*.

administration order – a court order made as a result of an application to the court by the directors, creditors and/or shareholders of a company for it to be placed in administration. The directors can also put a company directly into administration by filing the necessary papers in court. The aim of administration is to allow the company to be rehabilitated or reorganised if this is achievable or, if not, to ensure the most profitable realisation of the company's *assets* (see below).

administrative receiver – a receiver or manager takes control of all (or most) of a company's property. When a company goes into administrative receivership, an administrative receiver is appointed by the holders of any *debenture* secured by a *floating charge* dated before 15 September 2003.

administrator – the *Insolvency Practitioner* appointed when a company is put into administration.

antecedent transactions – transactions entered into in breach of a *fiduciary duty* by a director prior to the onset of formal insolvency proceedings. These can be undone or adjusted by the court. There are two main types of antecedent transactions: transactions at an undervalue and preferences (see pp 69–70 for details).

assets – the money and property that belong to the company and form part of its total 'worth'; the opposite is **liability**. A £1,000 car that is bought and paid for would be an asset; a £1,000 car with £1,100 worth of finance on it would be a liability.

associated creditors – the law recognises that, while companies are separate legal entities, they do interact with humans and other companies. There are rules showing how persons and companies related to each other must behave and declare their relationship. These related parties are called 'associates' and are 'connected' to each other.

Associates include the following:

o   any relations, including in-laws and step- or adopted children;

o   any business partner;

o   any company where a director holds with any other associate one-third of a company's shares;

o   any employee;

o   any associate of any of the above.

So, you see, it's a pretty wide definition.

bankrupt – an individual debtor (that is, a person rather than a company) against whom a bankruptcy order has been made by the court. The order confirms that the debtor is unable to pay their debts. The order also allows the bankrupt's property to be taken away and sold, and the proceeds shared amongst their creditors. Unlike the medieval bankrupt, they can still earn a living but cannot be a director or take part in the management of a company.

After the modern bankrupt has served their time of up to one year as from 1 April 2004 (before then the time was two years if the debts were less than £20,000, or three years if they were more), there is, unless there has been misconduct or a previous bankruptcy, an automatic discharge and, in effect, the bankrupt's slate is wiped clean. The state of being bankrupt is called **bankruptcy**.

In medieval Italy, a moneylender who could not pay his debts was *bankrupted*. He had his bench or counter – his *banco* – *rupt*ured or broken by his creditors. He was thus put out of business.

breach – law-speak for *break* (a law, a promise, etc); if you do so, you are said to be 'in breach (of Section XYZ)' or just 'in breach'.

charge – in this context, a claim on property or other *assets* that has to be met before other claims are considered. A mortgage on your home is the commonest form of charge.

claim – in this context, an official form on which a *creditor* tells the court what they want (usually some money you owe them) and asks for a judgment in their favour.

committee – in this context, a committee formed to represent creditors as a whole to supervise and assist the actions of a liquidator, administrator, receiver or supervisor in a formal insolvency.

company voluntary arrangement (CVA) – a private deal for the repayment of debts between a company and its creditors, supervised by an *Insolvency Practitioner*.

compulsory liquidation (winding up) – liquidation of a company ordered by the court as a result of a *petition* presented to it. This is different from *voluntary liquidation*.

connected creditor – see *associated creditor* above.

corporate – to do with a company (as opposed to an individual). The word comes from *corpus*, the Latin for 'body', and when you form a new company you receive a certificate of incorporation from Companies House.

creditor – a person or organisation to whom money is owed.

creditors' voluntary liquidation (winding up) – liquidation of a company which is unable to pay its debts in full within a period of 12 months. This kind of liquidation is started off by a resolution from the shareholders, but it is under the control of the creditors.

Crown debt – money that is owed to the Crown (ie, the government; the Queen is unlikely to be involved!). Typically this would be tax (income tax, PAYE/NIC, VAT, etc) or National Insurance.

debenture – an old-fashioned name for a written contract between a lender (typically a bank) and its customer for lending money and securing the debt on certain of the customer's *assets*.

A *debenture* is, to all intents and purposes, an IOU. The word comes from the Latin *debere*, 'to owe' (*debt* comes from the same root).

debt – this is where it gets confusing. The dictionary definition is 'What one owes to another; what one becomes liable to do or suffer; a state of obligation'. In insolvency parlance, *debt* is used to describe an amount owed by you (and the claimant is one of your creditors) or owed to you (and the individual or company is one of your debtors). Yes, this even confuses professionals. To get the meaning you have to take the use of the word *debt* in context. In this book, we mostly use *debt* as meaning a sum due by A (the debtor) to B (the *creditor*).

de facto **director** – see *shadow director*.

dissolution – the 'killing off' of a company. This is done by the Registrar of Companies in Companies House at the end of a *liquidation*.

Note that *dissolution* doesn't always imply lack of success; the word applies to any company which is closed down. Suppose you were an independent contractor with your own limited company, then you were offered megabucks to work on the payroll of a former client. You might well apply for your company to be dissolved.

distrain – bluntly speaking, to send in the bailiffs. The dictionary says 'seize the goods of a debtor'. The noun – the act of distraining – is **distraint**.

dividend – when all a company's assets have been realised, the money is then distributed among all the creditors. Each creditor receives a 'dividend', ie, for every £1 the creditor is owed, they might receive 2p. The dividend is therefore *two pence in the pound*.

extortionate credit transaction – Mafia territory! A deal which gives credit on exorbitant ('12% interest – a week!') or grossly unfair ('Pay in full by Monday, or the boys will break your wrists') terms, having regard to the risk accepted by the creditor, enabling the office holder to apply to the court for relief.

fiduciary duty – a duty to act in good faith and put the company's interests before your own.

Fiduciary comes from *fides*, the Latin word for 'faith or trust'. The coins in your pocket carry the initials FD, short for *Fidei Defensor* – Defender of the Faith. But there is a serious point: the origin of the word *fiduciary* has the aura of ancient codes of honour which still have relevance today.

file – to take or send a document (eg, a *petition*) to the court.

fixed charge – a form of security, in favour of a *creditor*, over specific assets such as bricks and mortar. A fixed charge stops the debtor dealing with (eg, selling) those assets without the creditor's consent.

floating charge – a charge or mortgage which a company gives over its current or 'floating' assets, such as stock, and it is free to deal with these assets in the normal course of trade.

Picture a river with the *assets* floating along like logs in the current. While the water is still liquid – until the *floating charge* crystallises – the company can buy and sell the assets that are subject to the charge without the lender's permission. If the company defaults on the loan, however, the lender has the right to appoint an *administrative receiver*. This is the moment when the charge 'crystallises' – which prevents the company from dealing in those assets. Then the river freezes and the logs are stuck in the ice – the assets are frozen. The administrative receiver takes control of them and sells them to repay the *debt*.

fraudulent trading – trading with intent to cheat *creditors*, or for any dishonest purpose.

insolvent – unable to pay your debts; owing more than you have. The opposite, of course, is **solvent**. **Insolvency** is the state of being insolvent.

'Solvent' comes from the Latin *solvere*, which means to unfasten, to unlock (like solving a crossword clue) or (in the sense of a *debt*) to pay. Money is like tap water. It's bad manners to boast about it, and irresponsible to waste it, but when your well dries up you're in deep trouble. It is this drying up that finally does for a debtor, hence the term *insolvent*.

Insolvency Practitioner (IP) – an individual authorised to act in insolvency matters either by a *recognised professional body* or by a 'relevant authority'.

in specie – a distributions *in specie* is where tangible *assets* rather than cash are paid out by a *liquidator* by way of distributions or *dividends*.

lien – interestingly, *lien* comes from *ligamen*, a string. A lien *is* a string, in the sense of a right to hang onto goods or property belonging to someone else until debts are paid ('I'll keep your car until you've paid for the repairs'). A lien can also be a form of equitable charge over property in favour of a *creditor*, who is allowed to sell that property.

liquidation – the process by which a company ceases to trade and has its assets collected in and distributed to satisfy its liabilities; the term *winding up* is also used.

Liquidation is to companies what *bankruptcy* is to individuals. Companies can jump into *voluntary liquidation*, or be pushed and have this move forced upon them by their *creditors*.

liquidator – the name given to a person who is responsible for dealing with the *winding up* of a company.

members' voluntary liquidation – this is where a solvent company closes down and can pay creditors in full and give the shareholders some money as well.

mitigate – to soften a blow or reduce the severity of something. In the context of an *insolvent* business (see p 75), an employee with a valid claim can get their wages paid by the government, but they cannot just take the money and run. They must mitigate that claim by at least claiming unemployment benefit and attempting to get another job.

nominee – the person named in a *Proposal* to act in the preliminary stages of the implementation of a voluntary arrangement.

office holder – a person who is acting as an *Insolvency Practitioner* in relation to a company.

Official Receiver – a civil servant who deals with the administration of *compulsory liquidations* and *bankruptcies*.

personal service – the delivery by hand of an important document by leaving it with the recipient (rather than using post, fax, email, etc), because that is what the law requires. Courts and lawyers serve documents *on* people to whom ordinary mortals post, fax or deliver by hand.

petition – an application to the court (in this context, asking for a company to be put into *liquidation*). *To* petition means to apply; *a* petition means the application itself. And the person who does the petitioning is called the **petitioner**.

preferential debts – picture a queue of debts waiting to be paid. Preferential debts are at the head of the queue. These debts must be paid before *floating charges* and before the unsecured debts at the end of the queue. Preferential debts now include only wages up to £800 and holiday pay due to employees. Before 15 September 2003 they also included PAYE and VAT arrears.

Proposal – a legal document which sets out for *creditors* the terms of a *CVA*.

provisional liquidator – a person appointed by the court to protect the *assets* of a company, after a winding up *petition* has been presented, but before the company is placed into *liquidation*.

realise – sell the *assets* of a company to raise money to pay the *creditors*.

receiver – the general term applied to the person administering any type of *receivership*.

receivership – the situation where a lender holds a charge or mortgage over a company's *assets* as security for a *debt*, the debtor defaults and a *receiver* is appointed to *realise* those assets to repay the debt.

recognised professional body – well, you wouldn't want a cowboy handling your insolvency problems, would you? A recognised professional body has the blessing of the Secretary of State. Its members are suitably qualified and licensed to act as *Insolvency Practitioners* – a safe pair of hands.

set-off – set-off is a common law remedy where two parties (either individuals or businesses) who are dealing with each other draw a line at a given point and one party pays the net amount in final settlement. In *insolvency*, set-off is mandatory so, if you owe money to an insolvent company and it owes you money, you only pay the net amount, ie, the amount that is left after you have taken into account the money the insolvent company owes you. Rosy calls it, somewhat irreverently, swings and roundabouts.

shadow director – somebody who, although not officially on the board of directors, still calls the shots. The 'real' directors act on the shadow director's advice and/or instructions.

The significance of this is that shadow directors are caught by the same legislation as official directors if they get up to mischief in any way. Professional advisers, such as accountants or solicitors, do not count as shadow directors.

A *de facto director* is somebody who acts like a director even though they have not been officially appointed.

special manager – a person appointed by the court in a *compulsory liquidation* to help the *liquidator* or *provisional liquidator* to manage the company's business.

statutory demand – a formal demand ('Pay up or else!') for payment of a *debt*, as the first stage of *compulsory liquidation* proceedings.

A statute is a law, and the law lays down the form which this document must take to make it legally binding: nothing else will have the same legal clout. A statutory demand must be made on the official form and *personal service* on the company is obligatory.

supervisor – a person appointed to supervise an approved *CVA*.

transaction at an undervalue – see 'Dodgy dealings' (p 67). This is where a company makes a gift or sells something for considerably less than it is worth, usually with the intention of helping the person receiving the gift against the interest of *creditors* generally. An *Insolvency Practitioner* can apply for such a transaction to be reversed.

unsecured creditor – the poor soul at the back of the queue for payment. This *creditor* does not hold any security (such as bricks and mortar) and will not get any money until the *preferential debts* and *floating charge* creditors have been paid. Typically, there is not much left for unsecured creditors who have no special property rights against the company.

voluntary liquidation (winding up) – see *liquidation*.

winding up petition – a formal request to the court asking it to make an order for a company to be wound up (put into *liquidation*). The equivalent for an individual is a *bankruptcy petition*.

wrongful trading – trading when it is obvious that your company is going down the pan! A director who allows a company to continue trading in such circumstances may be made *personally* liable for any increase in the company's *debts*.

Frequently asked questions (FAQs)

Here are the questions we are most often asked by directors of companies facing **insolvency**.

Liquidation

Will I have to attend a creditors' meeting?

Yes. At least one director must attend, act as Chairman and answer any questions that **creditors** may wish to ask (see p 55 for further details).

How long will the meeting last?

How long is a piece of string? It depends on the complexity of the case and whether or not many **creditors** attend. In most cases, a creditors' meeting will last between 20 minutes and an hour.

What happens if I am unable to answer a question that is put to me at the creditors' meeting?

You should explain that you do not know the answer, but will look into it and provide the **liquidator** with details after the meeting.

Will I be disqualified from acting as a director in the future?

Most office holders are required by law to provide the Department of Trade and Industry (DTI) with a report of the director's conduct. Where there has been 'unfit conduct' (see Chapter 13 for examples), the DTI may apply to the court to have an individual disqualified as a director for a period between two and 15 years, although marginal cases are not usually taken to court unless there is a history of business failures.

Are disqualification proceedings criminal proceedings? If an order is made against me, is this a criminal offence I have been found guilty of?

Disqualification proceedings are not criminal proceedings, they are civil proceedings, even though they are penal in nature in that they restrict your conduct in the future. It is better to think of them as an injunction – a formal order from the court – preventing you from being a director in the future.

If I provide an undertaking or an order is made against me, will it appear in the local press?

It is likely that it will appear in the local newspaper. The DTI provide details of all disqualifications to the Central Office of Information who will then alert local newspapers. You may therefore find a short article about your disqualification.

Can I be a company secretary after being disqualified as a director?

The answer is a definite maybe. The disqualification order or undertaking prevents you from being directly or indirectly involved in the management of a company. 'Indirectly involved' is an extremely wide definition. The larger the company you are involved in, the less likely you will be involved in management.

Will I, as a director, become personally liable for the company's debts?

No, except for debts which you have *personally guaranteed* (see p 20 for details) or if you've misbehaved (see pp 67–68 for details).

Will I be able to claim for wages and money owed to me by the company?

Yes. You have the same rights as other creditors. If you are a director/shareholder, the Redundancy Payments Office will usually reject your claim, but if you are paid through the payroll like other employees and you appeal, you may be successful.

How long will it be before the process of liquidation is over?

This will vary from case to case; although most of the work will be completed within a few months, it usually takes a year or more to finish completely.

Will I be able start a new company to carry on the same business?

Yes, as long as you make the best available offer for the business and **assets** acquired from the old company. You will, however, be prohibited from running a company with the same or similar name to that of the company in **liquidation** unless the business is purchased from the **liquidator**. See also the reference to 'Phoenix companies', p 71.

Company voluntary arrangements (CVAs)

What is the least amount that the company will have to pay creditors under a CVA?

Every case is different and there is no specific formula. The **creditors** will expect your offer to be the best you can make. There would have to be special circumstances for creditors to accept less than 25p in the pound.

Will the CVA be reported in the newspaper?

No, there is no requirement for it to be advertised – unlike **liquidation**. It will, however, have to be registered at Companies House and this is a matter of public record (see 'Useful contacts' for details).

Will my creditors want to do business with me? How can I overcome their reluctance?

This is always difficult, but they should be supportive, provided your suppliers are satisfied that you have done enough to ensure that the continued business is viable. You might at first have to trade on a *pro-forma* basis, where you pay up-front for goods and services.

What will happen if the company is unable to carry out the proposals?

This will depend upon the terms of the arrangement, but usually **creditors** will insist on a failure clause that would result in **liquidation** if the company failed to keep its side of the bargain.

I am not sure who all my creditors are – will that matter?

Although all creditors will be bound by the arrangement if it is approved, you need to make every effort to identify creditors.

I do not want to include all my creditors in the CVA. Can I deal with some separately?

You must provide a full disclosure to your other creditors of any that you propose to exclude from the arrangement. Only if 75% of your creditors agree are you allowed to deal with some creditors more favourably than others.

Company voluntary arrangements with a moratorium

In Latin, a *morator* was someone who loitered, dragged their feet or generally hung about. A moratorium puts things on hold; in this context, it is a legal authority to postpone payment, usually until a company in trouble can get its act together.

CORPORATE INSOLVENCY

When is a CVA with a moratorium appropriate?

Picture a small company (less than £5.6 million turnover or 50 employees). This company is under immediate, severe pressure from **creditors** but it is potentially viable if the backlog of creditors can be put on hold. The great thing is that directors continue to run the business with an **Insolvency Practitioner**'s role largely limited to fending off creditors. For this reason the professional costs tend to be lower than other **insolvency** options.

What is the advantage of a CVA with a moratorium over administration?

If you meet the criteria for a small company, then a **CVA** with a moratorium is probably better because you get the same level of protection up to the creditors' meeting and the directors continue running the company. This is as opposed to an **Insolvency Practitioner** running the company in an **administration**, making the CVA with a moratorium cheaper and less disruptive.

Administrations

I have heard that directors can appoint an administrator of their own choosing rather than having one imposed on the company by the bank – is this true?

Yes. From September 2003 it is very straightforward for directors to appoint an **administrator** if an **Insolvency Practitioner** is willing to act, simply by **filing** a couple of forms at court. If the company has granted any **floating charges**, for example to a bank, then the directors have to give the floating charge holders five days' notice, during which it can appoint its own administrator over the directors' choice. If there is a bank involved, the Insolvency Practitioner advising the company will usually consult with the bank and explain the plan going forward, to get the funding required in the administration before any forms are filed.

I thought that administrations were very expensive and only really suitable for large companies – so why should a family company consider this as an option?

This used to be true, but the whole procedure has been streamlined since September 2003, making it suitable for medium and small companies that are potentially viable but need some breathing space to implement a rescue plan or to achieve a better realisation of **assets** than in a **liquidation**.

A business in trouble

Meet the Licensed Insolvency Practitioner

In this book we refer to them as **Insolvency Practitioners**, or IPs for short, because unless you are licensed you cannot be an Insolvency Practitioner.

It may seem odd to start this chapter with a word about possible remedies for a disease, rather than a description of the symptoms. You do, however, need to realise from the outset that help is at hand. This is important, because nothing in the world will keep you afloat if your **debts** are dragging you down. You need expert help.

If you have toothache, you need a dentist – a properly qualified dentist; an amateur with a Black & Decker drill and a pair of pliers won't do. Be very wary of unlicensed 'debt counsellors'. You will find a great many of these if you type 'debt counselling' into your search engine, although to be fair, there are some worthy sites, especially those provided by government bodies, local authorities and universities (we mention some of the best in 'Useful contacts'). If your problem is debt, you should consider calling in an Insolvency Practitioner. Typing 'licensed insolvency practitioner' on your search engine weeds out the cowboys.

There are about 2,000 IPs in the UK, and approximately half of these accept formal insolvency appointments. Most have wide experience of personal and **corporate** insolvency, and employ a mix of accounting, legal and commercial skills in a wide range of situations. Many are chartered accountants like Chris and Andrew, co-authors of this book. Some, like Frank Brumby, another of our co-authors, are solicitors too. All are licensed to practise their art: a safe pair of hands, in fact.

An IP will review your financial position and set out the available options. These options may include formal insolvency procedures, and if necessary your IP can guide you into one of these and then take a formal insolvency appointment to continue to handle your affairs. Acting in such a formal capacity, the IP's job is to rescue the company or achieve a maximum realisation of your **assets** and then an equitable distribution to your **creditors** in accordance with the law. Unlike unlicensed debt counsellors, IPs are heavily regulated and you should feel confident that your affairs will be professionally handled.

If you are in financial difficulty, it is almost certain that 'no change' is not an option. You need to act to understand how you have gotten into the position you are in and plan your way out of it.

By the time you are thinking of consulting an IP you are probably worried, even scared. You may think you are on a collision course with oblivion – but actually it isn't that bad. IPs in general are a very humane lot because they are used to dealing with people under financial pressure.

There are other sources of advice too. Turn to your accountant, turn to valued friends, especially anyone who has had similar experiences. Borrowing more money could be the answer, but it probably isn't. It is far more likely that old-fashioned adages like 'Take care of the pence and the pounds will take care of themselves', 'Cut your coat according to your cloth' and even 'A penny hained is a penny gained' will bring a reversal in your fortunes.

What is insolvency?

You can find a definition of **insolvency** in 'Buzzwords', but no detailed description of its causes. This section of the book tells you what you need to know about the warning signs of when things are starting to go wrong. It really *is* a bit like toothache: many sufferers put off going to the dentist until the pain is unbearable. Regular checkups and the occasional filling would have saved a lot of grief.

'Annual income twenty pounds, annual expenditure nineteen six, result happiness. Annual income twenty pounds, annual expenditure twenty pounds ought and six, result misery.'

Mr Micawber in *David Copperfield*.

Mr Micawber was drawn from life. Mr Dickens senior was imprisoned for debt and 12-year-old Charles had to leave school and go to work in a factory. There was, however, a happy ending to this sad tale: the family fortunes improved. Charles completed his education and became a great novelist.

Insolvency, like toothache, always manifests itself in the same way. In the case of insolvency, you simply run out of money. If you type 'insolvency' on your PC, then use the thesaurus facility, you will be offered 'bankruptcy', 'liquidation', 'ruin' and 'collapse', which sums it up nicely.

Why might a business become insolvent?

Insolvency is the result of not having enough cash when you need it. To any insolvency advisor, cash is King. There are several reasons for running out of cash, caused by a variety of things:

o   trading losses through general bad/unwise/ incompetent trading or not adapting to changes in your market;

o   poor management of working capital, perhaps because there are several unpaid bills, or perhaps one big customer has not paid up;

o   maybe the directors have taken money out of the company which the company couldn't afford;

o   maybe the company has money tied up in machinery or buildings – money that cannot now be touched to meet the current bills.

In the long term, all businesses are there to make profits. If you are not in business to make a profit, you are either a charity or sooner or later you will become a casualty.

What about *corporate* insolvency?

When a company has financial problems, the causes may be the same as for an individual, but the effects are not. For a variety of reasons (see below), many businesses are run as a limited company. The limited company is a discrete legal entity, separate from the people owning it, running it and working for it. In a company, each of these people can be a shareholder, a director, an employee or all three. The company's lack of money affects everyone differently.

The *shareholders* own the company and have the power to appoint directors. A *director* has responsibility for running the company. Both shareholders and directors can also be *employees* of the company. But the company has a separate existence of its own. When the company makes a sale to a customer, it is the company that is contracting with the customer. When the company buys goods, it is the company that is contracting with the supplier.

A company's liabilities are notionally its own and no one else's. A director, or indeed other individuals involved in the business, can become responsible for some of the company's liabilities only if they agree to do so by giving, for example, guarantees, or if they behave 'badly' (see Chapter 13).

A word about limited companies

You can find out a lot more about companies in *Setting Up a Limited Company* in the *Pocket Lawyer* series. Here, however, is some general information. If you know all this already, feel free to move on to p 7.

Companies can be either limited or unlimited. An unlimited company is where the shareholders have guaranteed the debts of that company. This kind of company is a fairly rare animal and is outside the scope of this book, which deals only with limited companies.

A limited company exists where there is no such guarantee, or only a limited guarantee. This is one of the prime attractions for people going into business in this way – if they behave properly they are not *personally* liable for the company's debts.

Another key motive for trading as a limited company is tax considerations. The taxation regime for companies is not the same as for individuals. Companies get tax breaks that individuals don't get – and vice versa. Whether a limited company is the right choice for your business is not our concern. It is beyond the scope of this book to give advice on the subject and anyone considering incorporation should take advice from their own accountant. We will say, however, that at the time of going to press many accountants are advising people to trade through limited companies for taxation reasons.

Another reason for operating a business as a limited company is that the shares can be transferred, so new owners can be brought in or old owners can sell off their share in the business much more easily than if somebody were trading on their own or in partnership.

Larger companies are often public limited companies (plc) and their shares can be transferred much more easily and are often quoted on the Stock Exchange. Companies quoted on the Stock Exchange are able to have their shares transferred easily from one person to another. The more usual smaller company has 'Limited' or 'Ltd' after its name, not 'plc'. There may well be restrictions such as receiving agreement from the other shareholders before shares can be transferred.

Directors and shareholders

A company is run by directors appointed by the shareholders to run the company on their behalf. In small family companies they may be the same people. However, the duties and rights of a director are very different from the duties and rights of a shareholder. It is the responsibility of a director to run the company for the benefit of the shareholders: at least, that is true until the company appears to be **insolvent**. Then the directors have a responsibility to run the company for the benefit of the creditors – and this book deals with that stage of the company's affairs.

If the directors of a company are unable to continue trading through their own efforts, the company would normally go into some kind of insolvency. This book deals with corporate insolvency and corporate insolvency relates to the company only. It may have a knock-on effect on the directors and the shareholders, and obviously on the people or organisations to whom the company owes money – the creditors.

Shareholders have few responsibilities once directors have been appointed during the formation ('incorporation') of the company. They have the power to sell their shares and to appoint and remove directors. If things go really sour, their agreement is required to place the company into **voluntary liquidation**.

2

When is a company insolvent?

The answer to the question 'When is a company **insolvent**?' is not as straightforward as you might think. Firstly, you need to understand what the question is really asking – and that will depend on what answer is required! There are defined events that make a company insolvent and there are subjective judgments that make a company insolvent. When a company goes into **liquidation**, **administration**, a **company voluntary arrangement (CVA)** or has a **receiver** appointed over it, that company goes on record as being insolvent; it may well, however, have been insolvent for some time before this formal admission.

Here is an example of such confusion, taken from a conversation with an ex-employee of a company who had been made redundant prior to the company entering into a CVA. This employee wanted to know whether the company was insolvent. The answer was yes, it was insolvent, which is why it was entering into a CVA. But the CVA had not yet come into force. The company was not, therefore, in a formal insolvency and would not be so for a further month.

'In that case,' asked the employee, 'why can't the company give me my redundancy pay?'

The answer was that the company did not have enough money to pay him.

'But,' he pointed out, 'the company is still trading – and what's more, it's paying its existing employees. So surely it must have enough money to pay me!'

We had to explain that the company was insolvent because it could not deal with its **creditors** (including this former employee). It was only now able to trade because it could meet its (now reduced) overheads – of which his wages were one.

The situation is further complicated when a company goes into **compulsory liquidation** by having a **winding up** order made against it and the winding up process actually begins before the date of a winding up order!

So, rather than the one simple question, there are really three questions here. We would add at this stage that it is the job of a good professional advisor to work out what question their client is really asking! Here are those questions:

o   Does the company pass the insolvency tests (see below)?

o   When does the company go into formal insolvency?

o   When does that formal insolvency start?

The insolvency tests

Without getting too technical, **insolvency** is defined by two tests:

o   inability to pay **debts** as they fall due (known as the 'cash flow test'); and/or

o   the moment at which liabilities exceed the value of **assets** (known as the 'balance sheet test').

The cash flow test

Can the company pay its debtors if they fall due within the agreed terms with suppliers? The court rules that you have failed (or passed, depending which side of the fence you're on) the cash flow test if:

o   you owe a **creditor** more than £750; and

o   the creditor has issued a **statutory demand**, 21 days have passed and you have not paid up.

The balance sheet test

Are the company's liabilities greater than its assets?

Assessing the balance sheet test is more problematic. If you are in business, then your balance sheet should be prepared on a 'going concern' basis, with assets shown in accordance with normal accounting conventions at cost (what they cost you) or net realisable value (what they will fetch if you sell them for the best price you can get), whichever is lower.

However, by definition, if a company goes into a formal insolvency procedure it is *not* a going concern and at that stage the balance sheet has to be prepared on a 'break up' basis. So you value all your assets at what they might fetch at auction, and alongside you list your liabilities, including contingent liabilities like damages claims under contracts, redundancy costs and future liabilities under finance and lease agreements.

The difference between these two bases – 'going concern' and 'break up' – is like the difference between a delicious club sandwich and a slice of dry bread. However, if you are in doubt whether your business is a going concern – for example, if you don't have a credible business plan – you are pretty much obliged to assume that a break up basis is appropriate and, unless your balance sheet looks like BP's or Microsoft's, re-stating it on a break up basis is almost bound to show insolvency.

It's like going into a shark tank with a cut finger. The sharks smell the blood and move in for the kill. Once an individual or a company is insolvent, a turnaround or cure can be difficult to achieve, with credit that was abundantly available drying up and the available options narrowing fast. So you must take early action to keep cash – the life blood of any business – rolling in to maintain the business as a going concern and avoid insolvency altogether.

Failing the tests

It is at this point that the directors must consider the interests of creditors (as opposed to the shareholders). At this point, creditors are supplying the risk capital and the directors must respect that. The creditors are unlikely to be willing providers of such risk capital and therefore the company should only continue to trade if it is not at the risk of creditors. Broadly speaking, this would require trading at least at break even level without the need to increase debt to any creditors. Creditors must be treated fairly too during this period – the company should not pay off any creditors and should only pay for the *day to day needs of the company*.

So, going back to the ex-employee's query on p 7, the company could not give him his redundancy pay because he was not part of the day to day requirements of the company. He had at that point become a creditor and needed to be treated in the same way as any other creditor. The company could not treat him more favourably than anyone else.

During this period, the directors will be making decisions and taking advice as to:

o   whether they can continue trading;

o   whether any restructuring of the company needs to be done in order to turn it around; or

o   whether the company needs to go into some kind of formal insolvency.

When does a company go into formal insolvency?

A company goes into a formal **insolvency** by going into **liquidation**, **administration**, **receivership** or a **company voluntary arrangement (CVA)**, all of which have their own specific meanings that are dealt with later.

When does it start?

It is not until the formal insolvency that an **Insolvency Practitioner** is appointed and becomes **liquidator**, **administrator**, **receiver** or **supervisor** of a voluntary arrangement and takes control of the company. Up to that point the directors remain in control. To return once more to the case of the ex-employee, it is for this reason that an Insolvency Practitioner cannot deal with that claim until actually appointed and in office.

All insolvencies start on the day the company goes into formal insolvency – except when a company goes into **compulsory liquidation**. This is where someone – normally a **creditor**, but possibly a director or shareholder – rejects any other options and instead **petitions** the court for the company to be wound up. As we said before, a creditor will normally do this as a last resort when chasing a debt.

If this happens, there will eventually be a court hearing and the court may make a winding up order. However, the **winding up** is deemed to have commenced on the day the **petition** was presented by the creditor to the court. The reason for this is that the petition is a safeguard against the dispersal of **assets**. It is against the law to dispose of assets once a petition has been presented. The liquidator can go back to the date the petition was **filed**, in order to reclaim or rectify the position as it was then.

The time limits relating to various wrongdoings by directors (such as preferences and transactions at an undervalue – see 'Buzzwords' under **antecedent transactions**), commence from the date of the presentation of the petition and *not* the date of the winding up order.

Can you spot insolvency?

Companies in financial difficulty usually track a well trodden path along the corporate decline curve in figure 1. If you can spot the problems near the top, turnaround may be possible. If you don't spot the problems until the company has passed below the line, it will be hard to avoid some kind of formal insolvency.

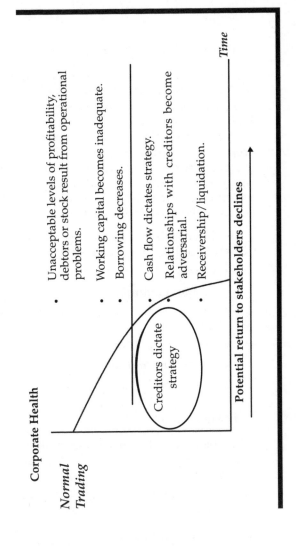

The Stages of Corporate Decline

Corporate Health

Normal Trading

- Unacceptable levels of profitability, debtors or stock result from operational problems.
- Working capital becomes inadequate.
- Borrowing decreases.
- Cash flow dictates strategy.
- Relationships with creditors become adversarial.
- Receivership/liquidation.

Creditors dictate strategy

Potential return to stakeholders declines

Time

How do you spot all these troubles creeping up on you? For Insolvency Practitioners, who come in towards the end of the story, it is dead easy to see the problems because they have the benefit of 20/20 hindsight. For a director caught up in the hustle and bustle of running a business, it is more difficult to spot trouble far off. There are, however, ways of alerting you to potential problems.

1 Know what is going on

Directors must remember that their main responsibility is to make profits for the shareholders, and in doing so they also need to look after the interests of the **creditors**. To do this they need to be aware of the constantly changing situation. Quality accounting information, prepared on a regular basis, is an absolute necessity. No company can be properly run without proper up to date books and records where at least quarterly management accounts are prepared on a timely basis – ie, within three weeks of the end of the quarter.

In the intervening months, key performance indicators (KPIs) should be monitored. KPIs may include:

o   turnover;

o   customer enquiries;

o   hours worked in the office or on the production floor;

o   outstanding debtors;

o   outstanding creditors;

o   cash at bank.

2 Forecasting

A business cannot run without forecasts or budgets or plans or, in the words of the late George Harrison's song, 'Any Road' –

> If you don't know where you're going,
> Any road will get you there.

When setting out on a journey, you would normally take a map and know where you are trying to get to. Even Christopher Columbus knew what he was trying to achieve and, therefore, when he bumped into America he had some idea why. Unless you have a map you will not know whether or not you are on course. Generally you will be off course, but it would be nice to know if you are doing better or worse than you planned. This will then help to forecast what will happen on the next leg of the journey, ie, in a year's time or (hopefully) over the next five years.

It is not sufficient to know how much your overdraft is at the end of each month, because when you start getting under pressure it will probably just stay the same – that is, up against your permitted overdraft limit. You need to know what your overall balance sheet looks like.

Recognise the warning signs

They say the spectator sees more of the game. This is true in **insolvency**. The warning signs are more obvious to a casual observer than they will be to you. When you are in the thick of it, punch drunk from fending off **creditors** and juggling your budget, what an outsider would see as a big problem may appear quite normal to you.

Pressure from creditors usually builds up gradually over several months, possibly even years, and therefore it can be genuinely difficult to see when you have crossed the line from honestly prioritising your financial affairs to recklessly incurring additional credit with no realistic prospect of being able to pay.

There is no definitive answer to this – and if you are in doubt you should seek independent professional advice – but see 'Traffic lights' below. If you are experiencing any of these problems, you may be near to or past that line.

Warning signs show themselves in various ways, such as:

o   getting further behind with your creditors, evidenced by red letters, chasing phone calls, being on stop and eventually receiving writs;

o   sending off your PAYE and VAT returns late and eventually getting penalties;

o   bouncing cheques at the bank;

o   shortages of goods on the shop floor;

o   perhaps buying an asset on finance that you would normally have bought for cash;

o   cutting down on necessary repairs; and

o   not looking after your staff properly.

All of these are obvious to an interested bystander, but they are not always easy to see from close to, especially for the busy director.

As we said, the spectator sees more of the game. Staff in the office and on the shop floor tend to spot the tell-tale signs well before the directors acknowledge the problem. This becomes evident when we, in our **Insolvency Practitioner** hats, talk to directors and employees. The true financial position of the company often comes as a shock to the directors, but when we talk to the employees they may have been fully aware of the situation for maybe six or 12 months. Directors need to take time to recognise the warning signs and address the issues. 'Traffic lights' below should help you to do this.

Traffic lights

 Go ahead but keep under review

o   You are unable to pay creditors in accordance with normal terms, but they appear to be happy to continue providing credit and services to you subject to interest charges and late payment penalties.

o   You are unable to pay arrears to the tax man, but you are able to pay current tax and have agreed a payment schedule to repay the arrears.

o   You can pay your creditors near enough on time, but only by increasing your overdraft facility or taking new loans.

o   You are not losing money and do not need more credit.

Proceed with extreme caution

o   You are not able to pay creditors within agreed terms and they have put you on stop, but they have agreed to give you longer to make proposals to pay.

o   You can only get limited credit from new sources and you are using this to fend off your existing creditors.

o   If you are in business, you can't accept new orders because you cannot get raw materials or pay for the overtime to complete them.

o   Your bank has decided to claw back your overdraft facility and you are having to miss payments to non-essential creditors. Your bank is putting you under pressure to agree to an independent business review.

o   Creditors are threatening legal action.

 ## Stop and seek professional advice

o   You are on stop and can't get more credit from anywhere.

o   You are regularly receiving county court **claims** and **statutory demands**.

o   If you are in business you are on stop with key suppliers, cannot raise working capital to fund your order book and turnover has dropped to below break even point.

o   With interests and penalties, your income is never going to be sufficient to meet your outgoings.

o   You are having sleepless nights and are on medication to steady your nerves.

Take it seriously!

Directors need to have drilled into them that *acting as a director is a responsibility, not an ego trip.* All directors are responsible for the running of a company and have a duty to know what is going on in the company. Those with specific qualifications, such as accountants, have an even higher duty, but every director has a basic duty to be aware and to be alert and to be responsible for the company's affairs. It seems incredible that people often burden their husbands or wives with this extra responsibility when there is no need to.

4

Who gets hurt in corporate insolvency?

The corporate veil

The corporate veil, as distinct from the assassin's cloak, is the protection a company gives to the individuals who are its directors and shareholders. The corporate veil separates the company as a legal entity from its directors and shareholders as individuals, and only in extreme circumstances will the courts allow the corporate veil to be pierced. Thanks to the corporate veil, a company can go into a form of **insolvency** with no effect on the directors or shareholders personally *unless*:

o   the shareholders have already contracted to pay more share capital than they have already paid, in which case they may be asked to pay the extra; or

o   the directors have given guarantees (more about this on p 20); or

o   the directors have misbehaved – see 'Dodgy dealings', p 67.

Shareholders

When a company goes into a formal insolvency such as **liquidation**, the **liquidator** will sell the **assets** and pay whatever funds he has to the **creditors**. Only if the liquidator can pay the creditors in full will the shareholders see any return on the money they have invested. As the company has become insolvent, this is most unlikely. In most cases, shareholders have paid for their shares in full, but it is possible that some shares are only partly paid for. In this case, the liquidator will be writing to shareholders for the balance of the payment due on their shares. If, for example, they hold £1 shares for which they have only paid 75p, they will be due another 25p in the pound.

In some cases, shareholders have not paid anything but have agreed to guarantee the company's liabilities up to a certain figure, usually £1. So, if the company goes into liquidation, the liquidator will call on them for £1. This kind of company is often set up for trade associations or resident housing associations.

Other than this, shareholders have no further liability unless they act as a director and behave badly. But, in an unlimited company (which for obvious reasons is very rare and outside the scope of this book) the shareholders' liability to creditors is unlimited.

Directors

When a company goes into formal insolvency the director is not culpable. The director has an underlying responsibility to assist the **Insolvency Practitioner** in getting to grips with the company and handing over the **assets**, but the director will not be liable for the **debts** unless they have:

o   misbehaved (see Chapter 13); or

o   specifically agreed personally to guarantee any of the debts of the company.

Beware of guarantees!

A bank in lending money, a finance company in agreeing to a lease or hire purchase agreement, or a major supplier may seek a director's guarantee.

Directors should think carefully before giving such guarantees, which go against one of the concepts of a limited company. If you do give a guarantee, try to limit the guarantee to a certain amount so at least you know what you are in for if the company should go bust. Try to prevent your spouse giving the same guarantee. Directors should be particularly wary of giving guarantees on finance agreements, as the penalty for *breaching* those agreements can be extremely high and may involve the total outstanding payments under the agreement with no right to keep the asset that was the subject of that agreement.

Creditors

People or ordinary trade creditors who are owed money by a company which goes into formal insolvency are generally the most severely affected. Normally they will not get paid in the short term and they may not get paid at all. Historically, in most liquidations there is no **dividend** to **unsecured creditors** and in only a very small percentage of liquidations are there dividends to unsecured creditors of more than 25p in the pound.

For the company that goes into **receivership** and eventually into liquidation, a dividend is extremely rare. However, if creditors are asked to support a **company voluntary arrangement (CVA)** there may well be substantial dividends (we will deal with CVAs later). If a CVA is offered, the creditors should think seriously before rejecting it because the other options are likely to be far worse.

Interlude: the times are changing

The Government addressed the lack of dividends in three ways in the Enterprise Act 2002, which came into effect on 15 September 2003. They did this by:

o   abolishing Crown **preference**;

o   providing a prescribed amount for unsecured creditors from new **floating charges**; and

o   refocusing **administrations** on corporate rescue.

It is too early to say what effect this will have, but even so, substantial dividends will be rare except in CVAs, or under the new administration procedures if directors take early action.

Employees

Employees will always be affected and there is a separate section on this, on p 74.

5

Strapped for cash

In many ways it would be easier if all trade were done in cash and no one ever borrowed money. This would largely do away with insolvencies altogether; however, in a market economy with enterprise at its heart, the giving of credit is an essential part of growth and business.

Credit and *creditor* both come from *credo*, the Latin word for 'believe' or 'trust' – (as in the Church of England Creed: 'I believe in one God ...'). When you buy something on credit, the supplier lets you have it in the belief that you will pay for it. So a creditor is somebody who has supplied you with goods or money in the belief that you'd pay what you owed. Sign spotted over the counter of a small grocery store in Tennessee: 'In God we trust; other customers pay cash.'

When a company starts trading, its net **assets** are the value of the money the shareholders have put into the company. In many small companies this may only be £100; in larger companies it may be several million pounds. Net assets are not enhanced by loans from directors that become a liability of the company. Such loans may provide 'working capital' to allow the business to function and may allow a company to pass the cash flow test (see p 8), but will have no effect on the balance sheet test (see p 9). We often hear that shareholders, in their role as directors of a failed company, have 'invested', say, £20,000 in the company, when what is really meant is that they *lent* £20,000 to the company as a **creditor** like any other.

Suppose you start off with £100 net assets. The company's net assets will only increase if a company makes a profit, assets are revalued (upwards) or further shareholder funds are put in. The reverse of this is that a company can only become **insolvent** on a balance sheet basis if it makes losses, if assets are revalued (downwards) or if too much money is paid back to shareholders, perhaps by way of a **dividend**. When liabilities exceed assets, the company is insolvent.

One of the effects is that creditors are now funding the company rather than the shareholders. By definition, when a company is making a loss somebody else is financing it, unless the shareholders put money in. So, if you continue to trade at a loss, it follows that you are borrowing more money from somebody, whether that somebody is a supplier, the tax man or the bank. You are therefore trading at the risk of creditors rather than shareholders, which is not the idea at all! This is the reason why the directors at this point are responsible to the creditors and not to the shareholders.

It is the job of an advisor at this point to explain this very carefully to directors, because what directors must *not* do is make the position worse for creditors. If they can trade at least at break even (in other words they are not losing money even if they are not making any) and the money owed to individual creditors is not increasing, they are doing no one any harm. To carry on, they will need to pay off some creditors, but this should only be an amount that they require from those creditors to continue trading, ie, they may turn the debt over.

The easiest mistake in the world is to keep your normal suppliers paid up to date and let the PAYE or the VAT debt increase, and believe you are trading without making a loss. This is why a balance sheet must always be prepared.

What can you do if you are beginning to have a cash shortage?

Do something positive!

'If you continue to do the same thing you will continue to get the same results.' That isn't what you want, is it? Be honest with yourself: take advice. The questions to ask are:

o   what are the options?

o   What are the likely effects of each option? *And*

o   are the achievable options the ones you want? *And*

o   are you, in picking a particular option, being realistic, too adventurous, too optimistic, too pessimistic, or straying into dodgy dealings?

It is a good idea to discuss these things with a friend or perhaps someone else in a similar line of business whom you can trust. If you start talking about your own problems, you will be amazed how many other people have similar ones.

Many people pay their accountant's bill last of all. Pay it first, because you never know when you will need your accountant's expert advice.

Whoever you are taking advice from, check their qualifications and maybe take some references or speak to someone else about the problem first.

Our constant cry to directors is to take advice sooner rather than later. We are not willing to be undertakers if we can be doctors instead, and it is amazing how our best advice is often advice that we do not charge for. When people ask us how we advise businesses, or what kind of advice we give them, we say that 99% of the time it is just a question of pulling someone's head out of the sand and making them face facts. In many cases, directors know what their options are but need help with seeing each one clearly.

In most cases, once someone has identified the options it is pretty obvious which one to take. Where the options are unclear, it can be just as difficult to make a decision to close a business down as it is to try to refinance it and turn it around. Closing a business down invariably involves extra loss, but where it is unavoidable steps should normally be taken to get the wretched process over with as soon as possible.

6

Turnaround

The biggest challenge is stopping, looking round and accepting you have taken a wrong turn in the first place. Any business can have a financial crisis – no business is immune from recessions, bad debts or market changes that can drive a whole industry onto another continent. Survivors know where they are and know where they are going. They have a clear idea of the problems they face and they have plans to deal with them. The earlier the problem is spotted, the more options are available. Look again at the traffic lights in Chapter 3 and try to work out where you are.

Answer the following questions:

o   Do you have a current business plan including profit and loss, cash flow and balance sheet forecasts at monthly rests?

o   Do you know your market, and do you know why your customers buy from you and not from your competitors?

o   Do you have meaningful and timely management information, including management accounts?

o   Is actual performance regularly reviewed against plan?

o   Does your management team meet regularly to formally review progress – or, if you are on your own, do you set aside time just to understand your financial position?

If you can answer yes to all of these, then survival is a realistic option.

The key is to have a plan and stick to it. When cash flow is tight your mantra is 'Cash flow is King' – but think of your **creditors**.

You have had the use of their money and they will suffer if you go bust. Most of what you should and shouldn't be doing is common sense, but here are some pointers.

Do's and don't's

Do:

o   Take stock of your situation.

o   Talk to your advisor or a valued friend.

o   Understand how you have got into your current situation.

o   Prepare a plan for at least the next few months.

o   Be realistic.

o   Act in the best interests of your *creditors*.

o   Ask your accountant or lawyer to recommend an *Insolvency Practitioner*.

Don't:

o   Incur more credit willy-nilly.

o   Lie awake and worry – share the problem with an advisor or a valued friend.

o   Prefer one creditor over another or attempt to hide *assets* from your creditors.

o   Ignore threats of legal action from creditors.

Acting in your creditors' interests would usually involve:

o   not incurring more credit (OK, not borrowing any more money!); and

o   taking steps to increase your income and reduce your outgoings,

so that you can repay the debt you have incurred.

So, what routine steps can you take to avoid informal **insolvency**?

How can you change the business?

Be ruthless, and don't be ashamed to ask for advice. Ask your employees, ask your customers, ask your friends, ask the bank manager, ask your accountant, and *listen* to everyone. Then ask yourself:

o   Are you enjoying this?

o   Should you be doing this?

o   Do you want to get out?

Don't let your heart rule your head!

So, having decided that you want to stay in business and that you believe the changes you are implementing will make a difference, draw up a plan.

Make a plan

Do a 12-month cash flow projection (see p 108), ask someone you trust to look at it, or indeed ask everyone – friends, bank manager, employees, accountant – to comment on your projections.

There is no point in doing a turnaround unless your plan is realistic. A failed turnaround is a waste of time and could expose you to personal liabilities. That is not to say that all turnarounds will succeed, as obviously there is an element of risk (and luck!). You need to be able to assess these.

What element of luck do you need? More importantly, what element of bad luck could you cope with? You may well personally have guaranteed the bank overdraft or guaranteed other creditors (see p 20) and the insolvency of your firm will cause your family embarrassment at best and financial ruin at worst. These considerations should not change your view, but they may affect your thinking as to whether you want to be involved or not. At the end of the day, it isn't worth doing unless it works.

A suggested list of items to consider in a turnaround would include the following:

o   recognise the problem and the need for change;

o   know your market and be sure you can give your customers what they want. Most highly profitable small businesses operate in a niche where they have little direct/local competition;

o   prepare or update your business plan;

- ensure you have meaningful and timely management information (including financial information);

- many profitable businesses go bust because they run out of cash. Understand your working capital needs and manage the business to maximise cash flow. We have made these points already, but make no apology for repeating them;

- sell surplus assets;

- collect money from customers – increase your prices but offer discounts for early payment;

- pay sales commission to employees when your customer pays you;

- reduce stock and work in progress;

- negotiate extended credit from suppliers in return for additional business;

- buy in management skills that are lacking – consider giving up equity to a 'Business Angel' – it is better to have 50% of a successful business than 100% of one that has gone bust.

Get on with it!

In a small book like this, and without knowing your individual circumstances, we cannot hope to go into detail, but consider these points and take professional advice. Get your head out of the sand and get on with it. Much of our job as turnaround professionals is doing just that: yanking people's heads out of the sand. You know there is a solution, you've thought of two or three possible options but you can't decide which one to take. Any one of these will be better than keeping your head in the sand.

A deal with creditors or new investors

Suppose you feel the business could be good enough, but you have just got too many **debts**. What is your next option?

An informal deal

You may be able to agree with your creditors that they will accept payment in full over an extended period ('Give me time, Julian, give me time'). In exceptional circumstances, **creditors** may even accept only part payment of their old debts (but see below for formal insolvency schemes to deal with this). If you have a few creditors, particularly those with whom you are going to continue to do business, who want to earn money out of supplying you in the future, they may well accept this sort of compromise on the basis that if you go bust they will get substantially less.

Creditors need to be persuaded to accept a deal and they are only likely to agree if it is commercially beneficial to them. Sometimes creditors will not accept because they want their 'pound of flesh', and they may want to see you go out of business anyway. Or they may be too big a company to cope with making a decision to compromise their debts. For example, government departments just won't be able to agree to a part payment outside a formal arrangement.

Your **creditors** may not get what they want anyway. The original pound of flesh belonged to Antonio, the Merchant of Venice. His deal with Shylock entitled the money lender to a pound of Antonio's flesh if Antonio defaulted on the loan. The judge ruled that Shylock could have his pound of flesh – hoorah! – but must not spill one drop of his blood – bad luck, Shylock! Many creditors since then have felt equally hard done by.

In order to do an informal deal, you need to set out to your creditors:

o   what the current financial position is; *and*

o   what would happen if you went bust.

You need to tell them honestly how you've got into this mess and why you think you can get out of it, and then lead on to why it is to their advantage to support you. It is normally only possible to do an informal deal with a fairly small number of creditors. An **Insolvency Practitioner** will be able to give advice on structuring an informal deal and hold your hand while you do so.

Advantages of an informal agreement

o   Inexpensive.

o   Re-schedules payment of debts.

o   No court involvement.

o   Avoids formal insolvency procedure.

o   No stigma.

o   Credit reference agencies are not always notified.

Disadvantages

o   Requires approval by all creditors.

o   Only appropriate where you have a limited number of creditors.

o   Not legally binding on creditors.

With this option there is no court involvement, nor is it, strictly speaking, necessary to involve an Insolvency Practitioner (although you may well find one helpful). However, in order to achieve full protection from your creditors, it is essential that all of your creditors consent to the informal agreement. The more creditors you have, therefore, the less likely it is that you will achieve 100% support. If one single creditor does not agree, then they may continue to pursue you for the debt until they are paid in full.

The problem with this, of course, is that the **creditor** who refuses to approve your proposals can often be the creditor who will wind the company up. There is no point whatsoever in agreeing to pay off the majority of your creditors, only to find that a few months later the company has been wound up in any event. In those circumstances, you will need to consider the other options.

If there are only a few creditors and the debts due to them are relatively small, then it may be possible to reach an agreement with those creditors by agreeing to pay each creditor a lump sum, or payments spread over a period of time. In order to do this, you should write to each of your creditors and explain your financial circumstances and offer terms for repayment.

Angels

If the business is under-capitalised and you need to beef up management skills, consider bringing in a Business Angel – you may have to give up part of your shareholding but it is better to have 50% of a successful business than 100% of a business that has failed. If you don't know which way to turn, talk to your accountant, contact your local Chamber of Commerce, or make contact with a Business Rescue and Insolvency Specialist listed under 'Insolvency Practitioners' in the *Yellow Pages* or on the R3 website (see 'Useful contacts').

Interim managers

You may not need capital, but you may feel that you need more experienced management. There is a growing band of interim managers with different skill bases who can come in and help you turn the business around on a full or part time basis. But check them out carefully first.

Interlude: honest failure

As we said earlier, Charles Dickens's father was imprisoned for debt. Whole families were confined in London's notorious debtors' prisons; babies were born there and old people died there. We have often thought that the concept of debtors' prisons is illogical, given that confining someone makes it even harder for them to earn a living, but the theory was that their friends and relations would club together to pay the debts and spring their dear ones from jail!

The bad old days are long gone. Since the latter part of the 1990s, the emphasis has been on business rescue and on giving both corporate and individual debtors a fresh start. More recently, current government proposals to reform insolvency law make their philosophy very clear. The proposals reject the proposition that a debtor, by becoming **insolvent**, ceases to be someone in whom society can have trust and confidence. Instead, they recognise that honest failure is an inevitable part of a dynamic market economy. You can't fail unless you try, and it is wrong to penalise someone for trying and failing.

The overall direction of government thinking is to encourage enterprise and move towards the US model that encourages risk-taking and sees experience of managing business failures as a core business competency. But balanced against this is a toughened regime of restrictions on **bankrupts** whose conduct has been irresponsible, reckless or otherwise culpable.

Company voluntary arrangements

Background

Company voluntary arrangements (CVAs) were introduced in 1986 to enable companies to enter into a binding arrangement with their **creditors** as to how their **debts** would be paid, or partly paid, and over what timescale. This was intended to be a company – rather than a business – rescue procedure, to give some breathing space to restructure and continue to trade back to financial health. However, in practice the CVA procedure has been little used, with about 10 CVAs in comparison to 1,000 **creditors' voluntary liquidations** each month. There are a number of reasons why the 'old' procedure was unpopular, but the lack of a moratorium period to give protection from a creditor enforcement action in the lead up to the creditors' meeting was often given as the main reason, though, as you will see, this is not always the case. So new provisions dealing with a CVA with a moratorium came into force on 1 January 2003.

The new company voluntary arrangement with a moratorium

The new **CVA** with a moratorium prevents creditors, including banks with **debentures** and landlords, jumping the gun, and for the first time brings the UK insolvency regime closer to the US Chapter 11 model. The key features of the new CVA with a moratorium are as follows:

- it is available only to small and medium-sized companies (defined as those with any two of turnover of up to £5.6 million, gross **assets** up to £2.8 million and up to 50 employees);
- the initial moratorium is for 28 days and this can be extended for up to two months;
- for the first time, **floating charge** holders, **Crown creditors**, landlords and finance companies are prevented from taking any precipitate action during the moratorium;
- also for the first time, unknown creditors are bound by the terms of the arrangement;
- the directors stay in control (subject to monitoring by the **nominee**).

What is a company voluntary arrangement?

A company voluntary arrangement (CVA) is an agreement between the company and its creditors. The agreement can be very flexible and directors will propose such an agreement where it is likely to be a better option for them, the company and the shareholders than another form of **insolvency**. The down side is that the creditors are only likely to accept a CVA if it gives them a better deal than the alternatives, normally **liquidation**.

The great advantage of a CVA is its flexibility and the way it allows the directors to continue running the company.

It is obvious that a CVA is not going to work unless the creditors trust the directors. In some cases, the skills of the directors may be inadequate (if they are up to the job, how did they get into this mess?) and, to persuade the creditors to accept a CVA, the board may need strengthening – perhaps by appointing an interim manager or a more experienced director. Of course, the reason for the insolvency may be a well explained one-off loss, and the creditors will be content to have their debts frozen for the time being and the company run by the same directors.

Every CVA requires a **Proposal**. The Proposal document unfortunately runs to about 40 to 50 pages and sets out the basis on which the arrangement is going to work. Much of this is very standard and provides the framework for the arrangement which explains how and why the Proposal is expected to work and benefit creditors. This is supported by current balance sheets and trading forecasts.

The Proposal has to be put to a meeting of creditors. It will be approved if more than three-quarters of the creditors who actually vote at a meeting agree to accept it (absentee creditors do not have a say). There are provisions to prevent **connected creditors** from pushing a Proposal through against the wishes of external or third-party creditors. Where connected creditors help push the vote through the 75% barrier, the Proposal will only be accepted if more than half of the external creditors who bother to vote are in favour of the arrangement.

A CVA is 'monitored' by an **Insolvency Practitioner** who acts as nominee in the first instance and is required to state that the Proposals:

o   are fair to both the company and its creditors; and

o   have a realistic prospect of success.

If the nominee believes this to be the case, the Proposal is put to both shareholders and creditors. If it is approved, the nominee usually becomes the **supervisor** to monitor the arrangement in accordance with the terms of the Proposal and to ensure it is properly complied with both by the company and its directors.

Insolvency legislation sets out a basic structure, but actual terms can vary widely. The kinds of Proposals that are often put forward include:

o   third-party contribution – where a third party, such as new shareholders, will make a lump sum available to pay creditors a **dividend** in full and final settlement of their debt, normally as a one-off payment;

o   voluntary contributions from trading – despite the company's past problems, if the business is viable and can make sufficient contributions from its future earnings, these can be paid into a pot administered by the supervisor to allow a dividend (or payment in full over a period of time) to be paid to creditors;

o   wind-down and cessation of trade – in some businesses the **realisation** of assets in a planned wind-down by the existing management can produce much better realisations than in a liquidation/fire sale situation. Again these can be paid to the supervisor to pay creditors.

Advantages of a CVA

A **CVA** is a formalised deal with **creditors**, as opposed to the informal arrangement discussed in Chapter 7. The advantages of a CVA over an informal arrangement are that, once the arrangement has been agreed, *all creditors are bound by it*. Therefore, the dissenting creditors can be bound into the arrangement whether they had notice of the creditors' meeting or not, although there are provisions whereby creditors who did not know about the arrangement can appeal to the court within 28 days of finding out, if they can show the court that they have been unfairly treated. This is primarily to ensure that creditors who could sway the outcome of the meeting are not deliberately missed off the mailing list to which the Proposals are sent.

The big 'plus' here from the company's point of view is that the creditors who are bound by the arrangement cannot take separate debt collection routes – eg, claim for debt in the county court, send in the bailiffs or present a **winding up petition** to liquidate the company.

Creditors have the benefit of knowing that the arrangement has been reviewed and, if approved, that its implementation will be monitored by an **Insolvency Practitioner**. This invariably gives greater peace of mind to creditors over an informal arrangement (see Chapter 7), which is not independently reviewed or policed.

Sounds great – how can I get one?

A director who believes a **CVA** is appropriate should contact an **Insolvency Practitioner**, perhaps on a recommendation from their accountant or solicitor, from the Insolvency Practitioners section of Yellow Pages, or by contacting the Association of Business Recovery Professionals (see 'Useful contacts'). The Insolvency Practitioner will discuss the options with the director and advise whether a CVA is feasible in their individual case. If appropriate, the Insolvency Practitioner will become the **nominee**, and will then help with preparing the necessary information that has to be sent to shareholders and creditors to enable them to make an informed decision.

The terms of the **Proposal** will dictate how involved the **supervisor** then becomes. Frequently their job is only to collect in, for example, monthly contributions, react if those monthly contributions get into arrears, and pay **creditors'** claims. In a larger concern, the supervisor may become more involved in the day to day monitoring of the business by reviewing, say, monthly management accounts (although it is probably best to keep the supervisor's role simple, otherwise costs will escalate). It can be as 'hands on' or as 'hands off' as the directors wish and the creditors are prepared to accept.

A term of the arrangement will be to dictate what happens if the arrangement appears to be failing, for example, if the monthly contributions are not made. It may be that the company will then go into a more formal insolvency, and if this is to happen there is likely to be less money available for both the company and the creditors.

Again, as with a turnaround, there is no point in entering into a **CVA** unless it has a realistic prospect of success. If a business is going to fail it will often be better if it fails sooner rather than later.

Creditors who receive details of a proposed **CVA** should consider them carefully and have an opportunity at the creditors' meeting to propose modifications to the terms of the **Proposal** to give themselves a better deal. A balance needs to be struck. Sometimes creditors may attempt to make the terms of a CVA so onerous that they are unfair, and directors must take care not to be pushed into accepting modifications that they do not believe they can deliver.

Will the creditors accept?

A **CVA** based on contributions can go on for as long or as short a time as the participants wish, although typically it is over a two- to five-year period. Where the **creditors** are likely to benefit from future trading, and believe the company is profitable, they are more likely to accept a CVA. In circumstances where the justification for future profitability is doubtful, they will be less inclined to do so. But the good news is that, once creditors accept the Proposal, the payments made under it will be in full and final settlement of their **debts**.

The Crown departments of HM Customs & Excise and the Inland Revenue have now formed the Voluntary Arrangement Service (VAS) to consider voluntary arrangements. Crown departments are often major creditors in small businesses, and their vote is usually pivotal. In order for the VAS to agree, they will want to see the best offer the company can afford and are likely to view a well prepared CVA favourably, except where there has been a history of bad compliance with Inland Revenue and Customs & Excise rules, and particularly where previous (informal) arrangements to settle old arrears have not been met.

Where these two departments represent a substantial percentage of the creditors (typically more than 75% of the total debt), they may take the view that the government has been unfairly dealt with in the past, and not be prepared to give the directors another chance. So a lot depends on the company's previous tax and VAT record.

Banks, who are also likely to be major creditors, are on record as saying that before agreeing to a CVA they expect to see the directors work hard and 'cut their coat according to their cloth' for the benefit of creditors, but a moratorium is only likely to be required where advice is being sought very late in the corporate decline process in very specific situations, where:

o   the company is under immediate threat of a winding up order;

o   its bank is poised to make a hostile **administrative receiver** or **administrator** appointment;

o   the landlord, Crown creditors or finance companies are threatening to **distrain** or take their goods back.

The types of situation where a CVA with a moratorium might be appropriate are summarised below:

Do

o   If business is profitable and cash flow positive but has severe cash flow problems because of:

–   a major bad debt;

–   overtrading;

–   loss-making non-core activities.

o   If business is not viable but an extended orderly winding up would benefit creditors.

o   If the bank, landlord or finance creditors are hostile.

Maybe

o   If business can be viable but not in the short term and then only if sufficient funding is available.

o   If there is a risk that creditors' interests will be unfairly prejudiced.

Don't

o   If business is not viable.

o   If business cannot trade out of difficulties even with a CVA.

o   If no trade-on is necessary.

o   Where a majority of creditors are hostile.

Company voluntary arrangements with a moratorium – the new procedure

The new procedure, like the old, is straightforward. The directors **file** the papers and statement from an **Insolvency Practitioner** in court and the moratorium is effective from this time. The moratorium is advertised in a local newspaper and the **creditors'** meetings must be held before the expiry of the 28-day moratorium period, during which time the nominee is required to monitor the affairs of the company, which is still run by the directors. Also, all the company's paperwork must state that it is subject to a moratorium

When to use the new procedure

For the first time, companies get some breathing space from their creditors' demands simply by filing at court – and they do not have to hand over control to an Insolvency Practitioner with all the intrusion and cost that that involves.

9

Administration

Historically, **administrations** have been little used and in the main reserved for larger corporations for whom the high cost of administration was not a problem. However, the **corporate insolvency** provisions of the Enterprise Act 2002 have changed this. With effect from 15 September 2003, a new streamlined administration process became available which has made administration a viable option for small and medium-sized companies.

Where a business is potentially viable or it is likely to be beneficial for the company to continue trading – for example, to complete work in progress – then administration probably is the most appropriate 'gateway' insolvency procedure to bring a difficult situation under control and create breathing space to achieve one of the objectives detailed below:

o   Rescuing the company as a going concern.

o   If this is not possible, then achieving a better result for **creditors** than would be likely if the company were wound up.

o   Only if neither of these objectives is possible can the **administrator realise** property to make a distribution to secured or **preferential creditors**.

The aim is to rescue companies rather than see them go to the wall. This is done through a collective procedure carried out in the interests of creditors as a whole. Administration is expected to replace **administrative receivership** (see p 64), and in some cases will replace **liquidations** unless the business has already ceased to trade.

An administrator can be appointed by a court order on the application of the shareholders, directors or creditors, or alternatively by a new 'out of court' procedure which is only available to qualifying **floating charge** holders or directors.

In the past, directors of a troubled company often had little choice but to invite their bank to appoint **administrative receivers**, who took over the running of their company and worked principally for the bank with little regard for other **creditors**. Today, directors can take the initiative and work with an administrator of their own choosing, with the primary objective of rescuing the company.

To appoint an administrator, all the directors of a company in financial difficulties have to do is:

o   find an **Insolvency Practitioner** who is prepared to act and who is able to confirm that one of the statutory objectives of administration can be achieved;

o   **file** a 'Notice of Intention to Appoint an Administrator' form at the court;

o   give any qualifying floating charge holder five days' notice to appoint an alternative administrator of their own choosing;

o   and if they do not, then file a' Notice of Appointment' form at the court.

Once appointed, an administrator has eight weeks to put proposals to creditors explaining how they wish to achieve the purpose of administration. Unless all creditors will be paid in full, or there are no funds for **unsecured creditors**, the administrator must call a meeting of creditors to approve the proposals within 10 weeks. Once the administration has been approved, the administrator must manage the company's affairs in accordance with the proposals approved by creditors.

Administration automatically ends after a period of one year, unless it is extended with the agreement of creditors or an order of the court. It can end in less than a year if the purpose of administration has been successfully achieved, or it is apparent that it is no longer achievable. If a rescue of the company has been successful, its management will be handed back to the directors. If rescue can only be achieved if creditors accept payments of less than 100 pence in the pound, ie, payment in full, then the company would most likely go into a **company voluntary arrangement**. If a company rescue is not possible, then in most cases a liquidation would follow if there was money available for unsecured creditors, or the company would be dissolved if there was no money.

How do I get one?

To get an **administrator** appointed, you must contact an **Insolvency Practitioner**, who will help you file the necessary paperwork in court, including a consent to act which confirms that he believes the purpose of the administration is reasonably likely to be achieved.

Beware! Not all **Insolvency Practitioners** get involved in **CVAs** with a moratorium or administrations. They could steer you towards a **liquidation** prematurely. If so, and if you think you fit the circumstances where a CVA with a moratorium or an administration is appropriate, seek a second opinion.

Members' voluntary liquidation

The procedures we described in earlier chapters generally affect the business of a company and how it operates; and either the company will carry on afterwards or it will have to go into **liquidation**. Liquidation means the end, the death, cremation and scattering of the ashes of a company. Once liquidation is complete, the company is automatically dissolved and it no longer exists. As the term suggests, the purpose of liquidation is to liquidate the **assets**: turn them into cash and distribute the cash (or what is left after meeting the costs of the liquidation) among the **creditors** and shareholders in the prescribed order.

Liquidation is used to liquidate solvent companies as well as **insolvent** companies. Although the term *liquidation* has been closely linked with insolvency, that is not its prime purpose and those who wish to liquidate a solvent company often feel they are getting caught up in the world of insolvency. These solvent liquidations are called **members' voluntary liquidations** and we will deal with these before we talk about insolvent liquidations.

The process

It may be that a company has served its purpose and wants to stop trading. This most frequently occurs with two kinds of companies. First, there are subsidiaries of large plcs following re-structuring or reorganisation of a group. The second kind is the family concern, often farming companies these days, who are selling up and distributing any assets to the family and/or shareholders.

An **Insolvency Practitioner** has to be appointed as the **liquidator**. The most important aspect of **members' voluntary liquidations** is the planning beforehand, and the Insolvency Practitioner will liaise closely with the family's or group's general advisors, and in particular their tax advisors. There are more professional indemnity insurance claims against liquidators of members' voluntary liquidations than there are in insolvent liquidations. The problems are usually caused by lack of pre-liquidation planning. The following issues should be considered:

○ Does the company really need to go into liquidation, or can the assets of the company be distributed to its shareholders prior to liquidation and the company then be dissolved by having it struck off the register? The Inland Revenue gives a concession to such distributions and treats them for tax purposes as though they were done in a liquidation, so long as any deal is agreed with the Inland Revenue before the distributions are made.

○ What are the likely professional costs involved?

○ What are the taxation implications of the timing of payments to shareholders?

   – Should payments be by way of **dividend** or by way of distribution?

   – Are there retirement relief issues?

   – Are there group relief issues?

   – What capital gains tax (CGT) might be payable on any property sales?

○ Are there any outstanding liabilities, such as warranty claims, claims under leases, legal cases that remain unsettled?

A prospective liquidator will wish to agree with the directors, who should be responsible for advising them on the above and any other issues outside the liquidator's statutory duties as liquidator.

To put a company into members' voluntary liquidation, the directors need to prepare a declaration of solvency in the standard form (see the companion website). This is a statement of assets and liabilities showing that the company will be able to meet all its **debts**, including statutory interest, within 12 months of the liquidation (though in practice the process of voluntary liquidation often takes more than 12 months, especially where there are complicated tax issues to be resolved). This document must be sworn in front of a solicitor; the penalties for making a deliberate false declaration include imprisonment. The liquidator will need to decide whether he or she is prepared to distribute monies to shareholders under an indemnity before all formalities of the liquidation have been gone through.

The company goes into liquidation in the same way as in a **creditors' voluntary liquidation**, ie, by calling a meeting of the shareholders, at which at least 75% of those voting at a specially called meeting approve the liquidation.

In many cases, all of the tangible assets have been disposed of and it is a question of transferring the bank balance from the company's account to the liquidator's account. The liquidator then needs to check for creditors (if they have not already done so) by searching through the company's records and also placing a formal advertisement in the *London Gazette* (details in 'Useful contacts') and any appropriate newspapers.

The liquidator will also need to obtain tax clearance that there are no outstanding liabilities. If tax has not been agreed, this can take some time. Without an indemnity the liquidator would be unwise to start distributing money to creditors or shareholders until all these points have been checked.

If there are any outstanding **creditors**, it is a wise move to try and pay them *before* the **liquidation**, as they will be entitled to interest at 8% on their **debt** from the date of liquidation until payment is made.

A liquidator is often hassled by shareholders to distribute the money early. This is unfair. The shareholders have made the decision to appoint a liquidator rather than distribute the funds before going into liquidation. In order to do a proper job, the liquidator must jump through the various statutory hoops and should be allowed to do so in peace.

After all the bills have been paid, any surplus funds will be distributed to shareholders, firstly by way of the return of their share capital and then by way of a distribution on top of this.

It is possible to distribute assets *in specie* rather than sell them off and distribute the proceeds. Where there is real estate or, for example, antique furniture, the liquidator would obtain a valuation and then transfer the item to one or more shareholders in lieu of cash.

Insolvent liquidations

The kind of **liquidation** we describe in Chapter 10 is a *solvent* liquidation. The kind we cover in this chapter is an **insolvent** liquidation.

There are two types of insolvent liquidation, which can be characterised as the one where you jump and the other where you are pushed. The first is a **creditors' voluntary liquidation** where the directors believe the company should go into liquidation because it is unable to meet its **debts** and the shareholders agree to place the company into liquidation. The second is a **compulsory liquidation**. This usually happens when a **creditor** who:

o   has not succeeded in getting their money by other means; *and*

o   is owed more than £750; *and*

o   can prove the company is insolvent (this is normally done by having issued a **statutory demand** which is unsatisfied),

then **petitions** the court to **wind up** the company. Unless the company can show that it is not insolvent, the court will generally make a winding up order and the company goes into compulsory liquidation (ie, winding up by the court).

Compulsory winding up

This stems from the absolute right of a **creditor** to petition the court to have the company **wound up** (or liquidated).

A **creditor** who is owed £750 or more can, in theory, force a huge organisation into **liquidation**. The said organisation would need to be foolish enough to ignore the **statutory demand** and also fail to respond to any of the subsequent sabre-rattling, but one day Jeffrey Archer may write a piece of pulp fiction about it. The moral is that an angry and determined creditor, armed with a copy of *Debt Recovery* from the *Pocket Lawyer* series, could give a troubled company a great deal of hassle at a time when they would prefer to be left alone to sort out their problems in relative peace.

What happens next?

The creditor usually issues a statutory demand and if, after 21 days, this is unsatisfied (ie, the debt is unpaid), the creditor then issues a **winding up petition** and serves it on the company. A hearing date is set by the court for about six weeks later and at the hearing a winding up order would normally be granted by the court, unless the directors can show the court that they are able to turn the corner and pay off the creditor, or strike an alternative deal such as a **company voluntary arrangement** or a **voluntary liquidation** (supported by a majority of creditors) to deal with the company's problems.

The actual procedure for compulsory winding up is dealt with in greater detail in another book in this series, *Recovering a Debt*, which is written from the creditor's point of view. We deal here with the effect on the company of going into liquidation rather than that of issuing a winding up petition from the point of view of a creditor. There are instances, however, where the company's directors can also issue a winding up petition against their own company. This is generally in a very small company when it may be cheaper to instruct a solicitor to issue a winding up petition than to instruct an **Insolvency Practitioner** to deal with it. As a rule, the directors will prefer to place the company into creditors' voluntary liquidation as at least then they will get a say in who is appointed to deal with it.

Be prepared

A company should do everything it can to avoid being served with a winding up petition, because winding up proceedings mean that control of the company is taken out of the hands of the directors. Once a company has been served with a winding up petition, there can be no disposal of **assets**, and as soon as the petition is advertised in the *London Gazette* the bank will freeze the company's bank account. The petition cannot be dismissed until the date for the hearing of that petition at court. This could be two months away – two months of limbo for the company. Meanwhile, once the petition is advertised, other creditors may join the petitioner and in order to dismiss the petition all these creditors will need to be paid.

It is far better to have spotted the situation beforehand and discussed it with an Insolvency Practitioner before a winding up petition arrives. All Insolvency Practitioners will be able to tell stories of initial meetings with directors who make out there is not much wrong with the company. Half an hour into the conversation, the Insolvency Practitioner becomes aware that the company has already received a winding up petition (this is taking 'head in the sand' behaviour to extremes)! It is still possible, even at this stage, to put the company into voluntary liquidation or get rid of the petition, but it all takes time and nothing can be certain until the petition is dismissed at the court hearing.

Enter the Official Receiver

If the court makes a winding up order, in nearly all situations the **Official Receiver (OR)**, a civil servant in the Department of Trade and Industry (DTI), is appointed **liquidator**. The OR has four months to decide whether to:

o   deal with the case themselves; or

o   ask the Secretary of State to appoint an Insolvency Practitioner as liquidator; or

o   call a meeting of creditors to appoint an Insolvency Practitioner as liquidator.

All of this takes time, and if there are assets to be dealt with in the meantime their value could go down. So, in general, where possible directors should choose to go into creditors' voluntary liquidation, because up until the liquidation they retain more control and the assets are likely to be sold for more money, more quickly.

In addition, the costs of a compulsory liquidation are generally higher than those of a voluntary liquidation because of the **charge** levied by the DTI of 17% on all asset realisations (up to a maximum charge of £100,000).

Another difference between this and creditors' voluntary liquidation is that whether or not the OR decides to have an Insolvency Practitioner appointed liquidator, the OR will continue to deal with any investigation work required in the liquidation. Otherwise, the duties of the liquidator are similar in both liquidations and will be dealt with in more detail in the creditors' voluntary liquidation section, below.

Creditors' voluntary liquidation

Closing the company down is often the least attractive option, but if, after all the other options have been considered, it is decided that **liquidation** is the best option, a **creditors' voluntary liquidation** is the lesser of two evils and will probably take a lot of weight off the shoulders of the directors. The Insolvency Practitioner, who is generally the proposed liquidator, will advise the directors prior to liquidation and will effectively guide them from the time the decision is made to put the company into liquidation up until the actual liquidation meeting.

This period is often called the 'hiatus period' and can be quite difficult. Creditors, as we explained earlier, are uncertain as to whether the company is in formal liquidation or not, and there will be a whole load of issues to deal with.

When a company that has been running for some time suddenly slams on the brakes and closes down, it is a bit like trying to stop a goods train at full speed. There is a lot going on and a lot of momentum. Should they continue to trade on a limited basis, perhaps in order to finish off some work in progress? Should they make staff redundant, and if so, how should they go about this? The staff themselves will need to be spoken to and the position explained to them. The directors will need to make sure they do not infringe any of the legislation designed to protect the assets of the company for the benefit of creditors.

During this hiatus period, the directors remain in control up until the formal insolvency meeting, although the Insolvency Practitioner will guide them through it. A brief list of do's and don't's would be as follows:

o Don't incur further credit that cannot be paid.

o Do try and finish off work in progress in order to convert it into finished goods.

o Do ensure that all expenses incurred during this period are paid for.

o Do deal with all staff redundancies in the appropriate manner.

o Do follow the advice of the Insolvency Practitioner.

o Don't prefer creditors over other creditors (eg, by paying off your mate round the corner).

o Don't take on unprofitable work.

o Don't sell goods to people who owe you money (because they may set the goods off their debt rather than paying for them).

Procedure

Following informal discussions, the Insolvency Practitioner will generally write a letter of advice to the directors. This letter should be formally considered at a meeting of the directors. At this meeting, the directors consider the financial position of the company and resolve that, after due consideration, it is not possible to continue to trade and that the company should be wound up voluntarily because it is unable to meet its debts as and when they fall due (see typical minutes of this meeting on p 91).

The directors then instruct their company secretary to call an extraordinary general meeting of the shareholders, giving at least 14 days' notice (unless 95% of the shareholders agree to accept short notice). At this meeting the shareholders will vote on whether to place the company into liquidation. In small companies the directors and shareholders are often the same people, but if not it will generally, although not always, be expected that the directors speak on the shareholders' behalf and therefore the shareholders' meeting is a formality.

Normally on the same day as the shareholders' meeting, but at least within 14 days of it, the directors must hold a creditors' meeting giving creditors at least seven days' notice of the meeting. In reality, therefore, the quickest time in which you can put a company into liquidation, having met the directors and made a decision, is about 10 days, taking into account postage times. There are provisions whereby the shareholders can immediately put the company into liquidation and the creditors' meeting is then held within the statutory 14 days (often known as 'centrebinding'). This would normally be used only where such immediate action is the only way of protecting the assets of the company. Where this is done there are restrictions on the liquidator disposing of the assets prior to the creditors' meeting.

Preparing for the creditors' meeting

Once the directors have made the decision to put the company into liquidation there is quite a lot to do before the creditors' meeting. Decisions may need to be made about the disposal of assets. This has been frowned upon in the past, but with proper professional advice it is often the case that a quick sale of assets on 'a going concern basis' can be achieved and benefit creditors rather than awaiting final closure and auction sale of assets. If a pre-liquidation sale is proposed, professional advice must be taken.

The directors must, with the assistance of the Insolvency Practitioner, prepare a report for the creditors' meeting to include a summary of the Statement of Affairs (see below), a history of the company, statutory information, a summary of the accounts and a deficiency account explaining where the money has gone. The directors are required to prepare a Statement of Affairs (see the companion website) giving details of all the assets and a list of liabilities to be presented to the creditors' meeting. It must be reasonably accurate and a director on behalf of the Board must swear that it is, to the best of their knowledge and belief, a full, true and complete statement as to the affairs of the company.

The creditors' meeting

At the creditors' meeting, one of the directors must act as chairman, although in practice the Insolvency Practitioner will run the meeting. The directors must present their report and creditors are given an opportunity to ask the directors questions. This is the one opportunity that creditors have to face the directors in an open meeting and the creditors are entitled to ask what has happened to their money. Honest directors have nothing to fear, but those who have strayed from the straight and narrow may be given a hard time by knowledgable creditors. It is an opportunity for creditors to bring to the meeting's attention matters which the directors may not have told the convening Insolvency Practitioner. There are always two sides to a story.

Creditors' meetings can go on for anything between five minutes and five hours.

The formal business of the creditors' meeting is for the creditors either to accept the shareholders' choice of liquidator or appoint a liquidator of their own choosing. They may also form a liquidation **committee** of between three and five creditors, who act on behalf of the general body of creditors to assist the liquidator with any difficult decisions during the liquidation. The committee has powers to monitor and question the actions of the liquidator. Where no committee is formed at the meeting, it will be normal for the liquidator to agree with the meeting the basis of their fees for the conduct of the liquidation (see p 61 for more about liquidation committees).

So what does a liquidator do?

A **liquidator**, once appointed, takes executive control of the company and the directors have no further rights with regard to the company, although they do have a duty to ensure that the records and **assets** are delivered up to the liquidator and to co-operate with them in their enquiries into the company. In most cases, the directors would assist the liquidator for a time with the disposal of the assets and the tidying-up of the company's records.

Briefly, the liquidator's main job is to:

o   liquidate or **realise** the assets; and

o   pay money out to creditors by way of **dividend**, in the prescribed order (after meeting the agreed costs of the liquidation).

Additionally, the liquidator has a duty to report to the DTI on the conduct of the directors in running the company.

Realisation of assets

A liquidator (as opposed to an **administrator** or a **receiver**) has very limited power to continue trading the company, and can only do so for the benefit of the realisation of the assets. The liquidator may, for example, complete work in progress where the finished product would be significantly higher in value. The liquidator may be able to achieve a quick sale on a going concern basis, with all the assets *in situ* and perhaps the staff still present, particularly if this has been explored and a pre-packaged sale set up. But more often than not the company would cease trading almost immediately if it had not already done so prior to the liquidator's appointment.

The liquidator will take advice from agents specialising in property, plant and machinery, etc, before deciding on the best way of disposing of the assets. They will need to consider what rights they have to sell the assets. For example, if the liquidator is selling the goodwill of the business, do they have the right to sell the customer database too? Are there any third-party claims over the assets which the liquidator is trying to sell? Are there any liabilities attached to the assets being sold?

Asset realisations: typical issues that may need dealing with

Freehold property

There may be a bank loan or mortgage secured on the property, so the liquidator will need to liaise with the secured creditor. If the value is less than the debt, the liquidator will leave the secured creditor to deal with the property. Otherwise, having taken advice from a surveyor, the liquidator will agree the best method of disposal and iron out any complications in the title.

Leasehold property

To get any value out of leasehold property the liquidator will need to pay arrears and dilapidations. Generally in short leases there is no value. Long leasehold property may be treated like freehold.

Goodwill

What on earth is goodwill? Goodwill is the value of the whole business above the value of tangible assets. It will include the customer lists, product information, brand names value, telephone numbers, *in situ* values, staff know-how and intellectual property.

Selling goodwill in a liquidation can be difficult unless there are competing bids for it, as it may be indistinguishable from the senior people at the company who may already have found new jobs with competitors or elsewhere.

Debtors

If someone has a query on a debt you can bet it will be raised now, if it wasn't before.

Stock

Stock is often of little value and is frequently over-valued on the balance sheet. It may be obsolete, in poor condition, or incomplete. In any case, it is expensive to move.

Plant and machinery

New machinery is cheaper these days, just like cars – why buy second-hand when you don't know what you're getting? So the price achieved in a liquidation is often below the book value on the balance sheet unless it has been fully depreciated.

Information gathering

The Insolvency Act 1986 gives the liquidator wide powers to obtain information from anyone who has information about the company that the liquidator believes may help with realising assets. The liquidator has the power to take court action and require a reluctant informant to attend an interview to provide information. This is called an order to obtain information and it is treated in detail in *Debt Recovery* in the *Pocket Lawyer* series. This may lead the liquidator to assets that have been removed from the company, or to recovery from fraud or misfeasance. More about this on p 67, below.

What a splendidly medieval word *misfeasance* is! So much more impressive than wrongdoing, misdeeds or, indeed, dodgy dealings.

Investigation

Although the liquidator may be seen as an adviser and even a friend, helping the directors of a troubled company to realise the company's assets to the best advantage, there is a sterner role too. The liquidator must consider the conduct of the directors in the events leading up to the liquidation and make a report on their conduct to the DTI. The DTI, based on this and other information supplied to them, will decide whether to apply to the court under the Director's Disqualification Act for a Disqualification Order against any director who is found to have misbehaved.

If the directors are not happy about the same person taking on both roles, they should consider taking advice independently from another Insolvency Practitioner or insolvency lawyer.

This point is dealt with in more detail on p 73.

Creditors

Having realised the assets and paid out expenses, the liquidator will pay creditors in the prescribed order as set out on p 75.

The liquidator takes control

As soon as they are appointed, liquidators have various duties:

o   to advertise the fact that they have been appointed in the *London Gazette* and a local newspaper;

o   to write to creditors with details of the Statement of Affairs and the report given at the creditors' meeting and any other resolution passed at the creditors' meeting, such as the appointment of a committee or on what basis their fees are to be agreed;

o   to report where appropriate to the liquidation committee at least six-monthly;

o   to report to creditors at least annually; *and*

o   to **file** six-monthly receipts and payments accounts at Companies House.

The liquidator has strict guidelines on how to invest funds under their control, and they have a set of powers to help them in realising assets and dealing with difficult disputes. The directors are not affected unless they have given personal guarantees or have misbehaved (see p 20 about guarantees and pp 67–70 about misconduct).

Beavering away behind the scenes

Like the swan gliding smoothly over a lake while its legs paddle furiously underwater, a lot of the liquidator's work is unseen. In a typical liquidation, there is a very active period a couple of weeks before the liquidation and a few weeks after it. It is during this period that most of the serious advice is given to the directors and most of the work is done.

Now the unseen work must be done. There may be complex assets to realise, or complex situations to investigate that have a potential for realising assets. Often this work requires legal advice and detailed investigation, involving poring over the company's records, and this kind of work takes time to resolve.

If there is money to distribute there are creditors' **claims** to be agreed. The Inland Revenue claim in particular can take six months or more to agree. This is generally quite a large claim in most liquidations and it is difficult to pay an interim distribution without that claim. There are also many more creditors who have not bothered to submit a claim and it is incumbent on the liquidator to try and search out those claims and, as a last resort, place public advertisements to disbar those claimants from current dividends.

On top of this, there is a considerable amount of procedural work to be undertaken. The insolvency profession is generally very heavily regulated and detailed procedures are in place to comply with these regulations.

Receiverships

There are three types of **receiver**: a court appointed receiver; a Law of Property Act 1925 (LPA) or **fixed charge** receiver; and an **administrative receiver**.

Court appointed receiver

This is a rare animal these days. In certain circumstances, an application can be made to the court for a **receiver** to be appointed over certain property of a company. The receiver is responsible to the court and must report to the court on his dealings. His duties and powers will be contained in the court order. This will generally be to **realise** and protect an **asset**, and he should have requisite powers within the court order to enable him to carry out his function. In all our years of experience, none of us has come across a court appointed receiver and do not intend to dwell on it further here.

Fixed charge receiver

LPA stands for Law of Property Act 1925, which gives the holder of a charge over a company's property a right to appoint a receiver. The Act gives the receiver very few powers other than to collect in rent for the building. He has no powers of sale and, if the property is to be sold, the charge holder will have to obtain a possession order and can then sell the property as 'mortgagee in possession'. It is rare that a charge still exists that does not give the greater flexibility to appoint a fixed charge receiver.

When a bank or other lender lends money secured on the property, there is an agreement between the bank and the company securing the debt over the property. This document is normally called a **charge** or **debenture**, and a well drawn debenture will set out the occasions when a receiver can be appointed and the powers that the receiver has in order to exercise his duty.

The right to appoint a receiver will normally arise when the company has defaulted by not keeping up with interest or capital repayments. There are no statutory rights to appoint a receiver other than those referred to above under the LPA, although most well drawn debentures will give the receiver similar powers to an administrative receiver.

These powers will normally include the ability to deal with the property and the business specifically related to the property. If, for example, the property is a public house or hotel, the receiver will normally have the right to continue the trade of that business. The receiver acts as agent of the company and takes over control from the directors of the specific assets. The receiver's duty is very much to the bank, to realise the property at the best possible price in their convenient time scale. The receiver also has a duty to **file** accounts at Companies House – but no duty to report to creditors generally or to the company.

Once the property has been sold the receiver would normally cease to act.

Administrative receiver

An **administrative receiver** is any receiver appointed over substantially the whole of the undertaking of a company, and the right to appoint normally arises in the same way as a **fixed charge** receiver when a loan has been defaulted on. The details of the loan and the charge are contained within a **debenture** giving the right to appoint a receiver.

The right to appoint a receiver, who is then an administrative receiver, is no longer available for **floating charges** dated subsequent to 15 September 2003. Administrative receivers will therefore die out; however, they will continue to be appointed in respect of old, pre-15 September 2003 debentures.

The duties and powers of the administrative receiver are set out in the Insolvency Act 1986 and they have detailed and considerable powers to run the whole of the business of the company and to sell off required assets for the benefit of the debenture holder, which in most cases means the bank. As referred to in the section on administrations, it has been considered that administrative receivers do not pay sufficient attention to the general requirements of **creditors** and, as we explained in Chapter 9, administrations will be taking over from administrative receivers.

An administrative receiver can be appointed at very short notice by the bank as soon as the necessary default in the debenture has occurred, although normally the bank will be discussing the situation with the directors of the company who will often invite the bank to appoint an administrative receiver. The receiver takes immediate control of the company and has a duty to write to all creditors within 28 days of appointment, and the fact that the company is in administrative receivership must be included in all company paperwork. The administrative receiver may continue to trade the company if they believe that the business can be sold as a going concern. They may well be able to save the business and sell it to a new buyer. Any surplus after paying back the bank would be available to the other creditors. In practice, however, there is little return to the other creditors.

13

Dodgy dealings

We have already described the concept of the corporate veil and explained that one of the reasons why an entrepreneur might choose to set up business through a limited company is that the company, not the entrepreneur, is responsible for the **debts**. This is the case unless they have given a personal guarantee (see Chapter 4) in respect of the company's debts, or become liable through the court being able to pierce the corporate veil to reveal their dodgy dealings.

The law is fairly tolerant towards honest failure, but deliberate dishonesty is another matter. Here are some of the things a desperate company director might be tempted to do, and the probable consequences of their actions.

1 Misfeasance

Misfeasance is a wonderful medieval French word meaning, literally, 'wrongdoing'. We all know that theft is a crime. The law allows an **Insolvency Practitioner** to take civil action against a director who has misapplied, retained or become accountable for any money or other property of a company that is in **breach** of any **fiduciary duty** in relation to the company. Examples of this would include a director using the company's money for their own purposes, or deliberately wasting the company's **assets**.

2 Fraudulent trading

If, in the course of the **winding up** of a company, it appears that the business has been carried on with intent to defraud **creditors**, the **Insolvency Practitioner** can make an application to the court for those concerned to refund the **assets** or property to the company.

3 Wrongful trading

You could describe this as recklessness: carrying on trading, using someone else's money, when it should have been obvious that it would end in tears. This section applies to directors who have given insufficient care to the interests of creditors when running a company. It applies after a company has gone into **insolvent liquidation** and where some time before this the director knew, or ought to have concluded, that there was no reasonable prospect that the company could avoid going into insolvent liquidation.

In this case, the court may make an order against the director to refund money to the company for any loss or reduction in assets since that time. This puts a duty on directors to look after the interest of creditors when they knew or ought to have known that the company was unable to avoid insolvent liquidation. In particular, they would be well advised to take early professional advice about continued trading in these circumstances.

4 'I never knew!'

The law states that there are two levels of knowledge that directors are deemed to have. All directors are deemed to have a certain basic awareness of the company's financial position, and those more professionally qualified (such as a chartered accountant acting as the financial director) have a more onerous duty to be aware of the company's financial position. But all directors have a duty to keep abreast of events. It is not an excuse for a director to say that they were not involved in the running of a company. 'Sleeping directors' such as husbands and wives cannot rely on their other half to fulfil this duty on their behalf. If you are a director, you have a duty to know what is going on.

John Selden (1584–1654) said:

> Ignorance of the law excuses no man; not that all men know the law, but because 'tis an excuse every man will plead, and no man can tell how to confute him.

If lay people cannot be excused, professionals are doubly culpable if their knowledge of the law is inadequate.

---

5 Transaction at an undervalue

Don knew his business was in trouble, so he sold the company Jag to his wife Susie for £100. Then he went spectacularly bust. Smart footwork, Don, you may think, but read on.

If, in the two-year period before a formal insolvency of a company, a director:

o   made a gift to a person; *or*

o   sold a company **asset** for significantly less than its true value,

the **Insolvency Practitioner** can ask the court to make an order to compensate the company and return those assets to the company. This piece of law would catch Don and Susie, as it was meant to do.

During this period the company must have been insolvent but, in the case of a transaction with an associate (for example, a close relative of the director), it will be for the associate to prove that the company was not insolvent at the time.

6 Preferences

If, during a six-month period (or two years to an associate – see above), a company shows a preference, the **Insolvency Practitioner** may apply to the court for the sum involved to be refunded to the company. A preference is where a creditor is put in a better position than they would have been in the event of insolvency, although the Insolvency Practitioner must show that the company was influenced, in deciding to make a preference, by a desire to put the creditor in a better position and did so intentionally. In the case of showing a preference to an associate, this intention is presumed.

This provision has proved successful in obtaining refunds from associates. However, it has been extremely difficult for Insolvency Practitioners to show that for non-associated transactions there was a desire to improve the position of the creditor. In other words – don't pay off your mates or yourselves.

14

Insolvency – common issues

Phoenix companies and use of business name

We have already learned that a director cannot be personally liable for the **debts** of an **insolvent** company unless that director has given guarantees (see p 20) or has misbehaved (see pp 67–70).

The Phoenix was a magical bird that, when it felt old age creeping on (as it did every thousand years or so), cremated itself on a funeral pyre, from which it emerged fresh and new and ready for another thousand years of adventures.

Some companies are like the Phoenix, as you will see. There is nothing in law to prevent a former director of a struggling company from buying the **assets** of that company from an **Insolvency Practitioner** – or indeed, if this is done correctly, from buying the assets of the company before it becomes insolvent – and trading again either personally or through another limited company.

However, where a company is insolvent, the director has a duty, as we have already seen, to consider the interests of the **creditors** of the company. So, if the director proposes to purchase the assets, they should do so at full market value and above the price for which an Insolvency Practitioner could sell the assets.

When this kind of manoeuvre is done properly, there is nothing wrong with it, but there is still a public perception that such sales are unsavoury. This strengthens the view that not only must the assets be sold at the right price, but they must *be seen to be sold* at the right price. Directors considering such action should take professional advice.

With the creditors' interests in mind, the law places certain restrictions concerning the use of a company's name in future. When a company has become insolvent, a director is not usually allowed to use a name the same as, or similar to, that of the insolvent company. The exceptions are:

o when a company with a similar name continues to trade and has been trading for at least 12 months before the insolvency; *or*

o where directors themselves, or a limited company of which they are directors, have purchased the assets from an Insolvency Practitioner *and* all of the creditors have been given details of the sale; *or*

o where the director has obtained the authority of the court to use the same or similar name.

Beware – if you use a similar name and the exceptions don't apply, you are committing a criminal offence.

The Department of Trade and Industry will not look favourably on future failures by the same director through a 'Phoenix' company.

Directors, shadow directors and *de facto* directors

Companies are usually run by their directors, who are formally appointed and have their details registered at Companies House. However, a person can also be a **shadow director**, a sort of *eminence grise* who calls all the shots and gives instructions to the board of directors. Similarly, a *de facto* **director** is someone who holds himself out or acts as a director although not formally appointed, and is therefore not in the Companies House records.

Both shadow and *de facto* directors have the same responsibilities as officially appointed directors, in the sense that they are subject to the same penalties if the company goes bust.

De facto is Latin for 'in fact', and a *de facto* director, ruler or whatever, is the boss in all but name. We all know organisations which are run by someone other than the name on the letterhead. The MD's secretary may be a strong contender ...

Director's disqualification

When a company becomes insolvent through an **administration**, a **liquidation** or an **administrative receivership**, the appointed Insolvency Practitioner has a duty to consider whether or not to make a report to the Department of Trade and Industry (DTI) on whether that person is unfit to be a director of a company. Based on this report, the DTI will consider whether to apply to court for the director's disqualification.

Rogue doctors and solicitors get struck off; dishonest (or incompetent) directors get disqualified. The Company Directors Disqualification Act 1986 sets out the various sins for which a company director can be disqualified. These range from failure to **file** accounts to running the company without due care for its creditors.

For selfish reasons only there is another reason to know whether your company can still pass the insolvency tests (see p 8). We said you must look after creditors – and this means all creditors. It is no good only paying your pushy or vital suppliers – you must keep the taxman up to date. To ignore the Inland Revenue is a sure sign of not treating all creditors fairly (and a sure sign that you will fail the cash flow test, as you can't pay your taxes).

Obviously, involvement in dodgy dealings (see pp 67–70) will normally warrant an unfit conduct report.

The DTI has two years from the date of formal insolvency to decide whether to take disqualification proceedings against you. It is now possible to give the

DTI an 'undertaking', ie, plead guilty before you get to court and agree what period of disqualification you are prepared to accept. This will avoid much of the expense of a court hearing. If you believe you may be disqualified, you need to take specialist insolvency legal advice at an early stage.

During a period of disqualification (a minimum of two years and a maximum of 15 years), a director is unable to take part in the formation, management or running of a limited company. It is a criminal offence if you **breach** the terms of disqualification.

There is also an element of public humiliation here. The List of Disqualified Directors is kept at Companies House. Anyone can call the Disqualified Directors Register on the general helpline (0870 3333636) giving the person's surname and initial; they can usually check over the telephone. The List can also be accessed on the Companies House website (see 'Useful contacts' for details).

Employee issues

When a firm goes bust, the workforce is of course affected. In a formal insolvency, the law gives employees special status. Certain of their claims are **preferential** and therefore rank ahead of the bank and its claim under the **floating charge**. Additionally, some of their claims are guaranteed by the Redundancy Payments Office of the Secretary of State for Trade and Industry. See 'Useful contacts' for their details.

Where the DTI has paid out money to an employee, the DTI will then step into the shoes of the employee as far as their claim would have been in the insolvency of the company. Suppose David Copperfield is owed wages by Wickfield and Company, which is going bust. David would suffer severe hardship if he did not receive any wages. The DTI steps in and pays him some money according to a strict formula – see below. While David gets on with his life, the DTI joins the queue of creditors on his behalf. This can get fairly complicated, but David gets his money while everyone else is arguing the toss …

Claims guaranteed by the DTI

The DTI will guarantee the following claims up to a maximum, currently set at £270 gross pay per week:

o   any arrears of wages owing to the employee in the six-week period prior to the insolvency;

o   any arrears of holiday pay earned but not taken;

o   claims for redundancy, which are calculated in accordance with a special table, and work out at one to one-and-a-half weeks for every year worked up to 20 years;

o   any claims for statutory pay in lieu of notice, which is calculated as one week for every year of service up to a maximum of 12 weeks.

The law regards this as a claim for damages, which must be **mitigated**. In other words, an employee with a valid claim cannot just take the money and run off on holiday. They must mitigate that claim by at least claiming unemployment benefit and attempting to get another job. Any money they get in this way will be deducted from their claim because they will not have suffered any loss in respect of those extra earnings. The DTI will in any event deduct unemployment benefit and assume that it has been claimed, even if the employee never gets around to filling in the forms!

Another title in the *Pocket Lawyer* series, *Your Rights at Work*, sets out in detail an employee's rights if their employer goes bust.

The queue – priority of claims in insolvency

At the head of the queue are:

o   Any secured creditors who have not been paid out of **assets** over which they have a **charge**, for example, a bank with a loan on a property or a factoring company with an assignment on the book debts.

Next in line:

o Preferential creditors – broadly speaking, employees. Any arrears of wages up to £800 and any amount owed for holiday pay that employees have earned but not yet taken count as preferential. Note that arrears of PAYE and VAT within certain limits were also preferential up until 15 September 2003. After that date they – in effect the Revenue and HM Customs & Excise – were ushered to the back of the queue with the **unsecured creditors**.

Note also that where the DTI has paid out money to any employee see (pp 74–75 for how this works), it will take equal precedence with employees.

o The reserved fund is a new kid on the block. It only applies where the floating charge (see below) is dated *on or after 15 September 2003*. The aim of this fund is to put the banks in no better position than they were when preferential creditors included PAYE and VAT. With this in mind, the **liquidator** must make available a prescribed amount to the unsecured creditors before making any payment to floating charge holders – see the next point, below. The purpose is to provide at least some money for the unsecured creditors. The reserved fund is calculated as follows:

– 50% of the first £10,000 of the net funds available;

– 20% thereafter;

– up to a maximum fund of £600,000.

o Any amounts due under a floating charge security. This will generally be where a bank or other person or organisation has lent money secured by a floating charge, and a floating charge would normally be over general plant and equipment, stock and debtors.

o Unsecured creditors: at the back of the queue are the unsecured creditors, who will include:

– general trade creditors;

– PAYE and VAT (newly demoted – see above);

– any amounts owing to the directors;

- any shortfall on the finance agreements; *and*
- any amounts owing to employees over and above those included in the preferential creditors (see above).

o Statutory interest – if, in a liquidation, there is sufficient money to pay the above in full (very unlikely), all creditors are entitled to statutory interest, currently set at 8% per annum from the date of liquidation until the date the debt is paid.

History note

Until the Enterprise Act 2002 came into force, the Revenue and the VAT man were preferential creditors. They now rank equally with the one-man firm who installed the office IT system, but they still have considerably more clout – and certainly better access to expert advice.

Distraint

Landlords through the ages have acquired substantial rights for debts owing to them, and to **distrain** – to seize someone's **assets** to pay a debt – is one of them.

If your home or business accommodation is rented, and the rent is in arrears, the landlord may distrain on the company's assets that are located within the rented property. There are complex, old-fashioned rules concerning this, but basically a landlord can only distrain if they can obtain entry without force during the hours of daylight – so midnight raids are not on.

In some circumstances a landlord can distrain both before and after a **creditors' voluntary liquidation** and can therefore jump the queue and gain an advantage over other creditors. In **compulsory liquidation**, however, the landlord is more restricted unless they distrain three months before the **petition** is presented, which would seem to demand considerable farsightedness or some impressive rent arrears.

A landlord can also forfeit the lease by obtaining re-entry into the building (this is an alternative option to distraining, and the landlord must decide which option to use because they cannot distrain after forfeiting the lease, although in practice possession is still nine-tenths of the law!). The landlord can then claim in the liquidation for any liabilities due under the remainder of the lease, both in respect of outstanding rent right to the end of the lease and any repairs due under the lease.

Recent court cases have, however, confirmed that it is the landlord's duty, like an employee's, to mitigate their claim by re-letting the premises, and it is normally assumed that a landlord should be able to do this within two years. So it is general practice to allow up to two years' future rent as a claim in the liquidation.

Who else can distrain?

Suppose you owe money to:

○   the Inland Revenue;

○   the VAT man;

○   the local council for rates; *or*

○   a creditor who has obtained judgment for debt in a court.

All of these have the right under general law to seize a company's assets, but they are different from the landlord in one respect. A company is fair game while it is frantically treading water, but once it has entered into formal insolvency, nobody except the landlord (see above) has the right to distrain.

Distraint by a private bailiff instructed by a **creditor** with a court judgment can be overturned by putting the company into **liquidation** before the goods are sold and paid to the creditor. So if the liquidation is certain and the bailiffs have just distrained you can make these goods available to creditors generally by putting the company into liquidation – contact an **Insolvency Practitioner** at this point.

CORPORATE INSOLVENCY

Liens

Certain classes of **creditor** are allowed to take a **lien** over **assets** in their hands. A lien is a right to retain an asset of the company and sell it to offset any debt owing. Examples of liens are:

o   a haulier's lien – a transporter who is carrying goods belonging to a company can keep those goods to meet the costs of a bill in respect of those goods. They cannot, however, keep goods to pay *other* debts which that company owes them unless they have that right under a specific contract, which – surprise, surprise – most hauliers have in their terms and conditions of trade;

o   a repairer's lien – a garage can hang onto a vehicle and sell it to meet the repair bills of that vehicle but, just like a haulier, they can only use it to meet the bills relating to that vehicle.

Committees

In all formal insolvencies, the **creditors** have the right to appoint a **committee**. The general purpose of a committee is to act as a sounding board for the **Insolvency Practitioner** during the conduct of the insolvency.

Formation

The committee in a liquidation is normally formed at the first meeting of creditors. In a **company voluntary arrangement (CVA)** it will normally be agreed at the meeting to consider the company's proposals, and in an **administration** or **administrative receivership** it is also normally called at the first meeting, which is generally held two to three months after the administration or administrative receivership starts.

The committee must consist of three, four or five representatives of creditors. The rule is strictly 'one man one vote'; no one person can represent more than one creditor and no creditor can have more than one representative.

The role of committee members is to represent the general body of creditors and not their own specific interests. There are restrictions on committee members dealing with any of the assets of the company. Committee members are unpaid but may be paid their expenses for attending committee meetings.

Functions

In a complex case, the liquidator may have to decide whether to spend time, and therefore money, on speculative investigations with a view to enhancing the value of the assets. They will want to have the committee's agreement to do so. The committee may well know more about the affairs of the company than the liquidator does, and will thus be able to help and advise. The liquidator must hold committee meetings as agreed by the committee, and must report to them at least every six months. The committee can agree to have meetings by post rather than physically; this is their choice.

Powers

The committee cannot force their wishes on to the liquidator, but they do have powers to require the liquidator to report to them and to be able to inspect certain of the liquidator's records. Any creditor who becomes a committee member will be sent a standard booklet setting out the committee's duties, responsibilities and powers.

It is not generally an onerous task and can be very useful for a liquidator in a complex liquidation.

15

You and your insolvency practitioner – and a word of encouragement

In an ideal world, as soon as you felt that you or your company faced financial trouble, you would get advice at an early stage. An **Insolvency Practitioner (IP)** would be able to tell you the various options involved, and help you to choose the best option for you.

Many directors have a good relationship with their accountants or solicitors, who will be able to provide the names of two or three local IPs. Failing personal recommendation, the Association of Business Recovery Professionals (R3) provides a list of Insolvency Practitioners in local areas and most Yellow Pages have a section sponsored by R3 in your area. See 'Useful contacts' for details.

Most Insolvency Practitioners will provide free initial consultations.

Many relationships involve 'good faith'. But an IP's duty is one of 'utmost good faith' – *uberrimae fidei*. This demands the highest standards of integrity. The IP must be not only clean, but squeaky clean, and what's more, must be seen to be clean.

Before accepting an appointment, the IP must consider ethical guidelines laid down by their governing body, and must act with and maintain:

- o   integrity;
- o   independence; *and*
- o   objectivity.

The IP is nobody's poodle and must not accept an appointment where a potential conflict of interest exists. In other words, will taking the job put the IP in an awkward position either professionally or personally? In particular, an IP should not accept an appointment where there has been a 'material professional relationship' within three years prior to the appointment. This would normally prevent your accountant from taking on the job.

If you are concerned that the IP cannot comply with their ethical guidelines, you must raise your concerns with them to enable them to consider your concerns and respond accordingly. If you are not satisfied with the response, then you should either shop elsewhere if it is not too late, or consider raising the problem with the IP's professional body (see 'Useful contacts').

Some decisions that IPs have to take require approval from the creditors' **committee**, the creditors or the Department of Trade and Industry (DTI). So, although IPs have a great deal of power, they do not have a totally free hand. For example, in a **compulsory liquidation** agreement is required to take legal proceedings.

Complaints about an Insolvency Practitioner

What if you have a grievance against an **Insolvency Practitioner**? If you are unhappy in any way with the way the IP is managing your affairs, then you should start by raising your concerns with them as soon as possible.

If you are not satisfied, then two courses of action are available to you:

- o   Complain to the IP's governing body – see above.
- o   Make an application to court. The court is the ultimate decision-making body and has the power to approve or vary certain decisions of the IP.

However, the court will not generally interfere where the IP has exercised their discretion properly. It is difficult to summarise when the court will and will not interfere, and you are best seeking legal advice.

As with any complaint, it is always best to approach the IP personally. For example, a common grievance is apparent slowness in answering letters. The answer may well be that the IP is often at the mercy of other people, who may not appreciate the urgency of your case.

If a personal approach does not get the result you want, you should consider writing to the IPs' professional body, who will take your complaint seriously and demand answers from your IP. Of course, the answers may not be the ones you were hoping for – see below.

It is easy to find out who to complain to. All IPs must state on their correspondence which RPBs license them. So check your IP's letterhead, then consult 'Useful contacts'.

Is it in fact worth complaining? Insolvency is an area where there are a lot of conflicting points of view and Insolvency Practitioners are required to deal with these in accordance with the law and their professional standards. People with a grievance should consider whether they are genuinely being treated unfairly, or whether they are, in effect, simply shooting the messenger for bringing unwelcome news.

Typical complaints concern the level of fees. In any form of insolvency the Insolvency Practitioner agrees the basis of their fees with the relevant people, ie:

o   pre-insolvency – with the directors;

o   members' liquidation – with the shareholders;

o   formal insolvency – with the creditors,

and when agreeing the basis for fees the IP should write to all creditors or shareholders setting out:

o   the basis upon which they will be charging fees;

o   the basis for agreeing those fees with creditors;

o   the procedures that creditors have to challenge those fees; and

o   relevant charge out rates.

A Guide to Insolvency Practitioners' Fees must be sent to all creditors with the notice calling any meeting at which the basis of his fees is to be agreed. You can get a copy of this from the IP or download one from the R3 website (see 'Useful contacts'). If your IP is not sticking to these guidelines, you probably have cause for complaint. Otherwise, however astronomical their fees may seem to you, there is nothing you can do.

A word of encouragement

All insolvencies mean a lot of stress for the people involved. The most anxious time will be the months leading up to the actual **insolvency**, and many people feel a great sense of relief once the responsibility for their or their company's affairs has been passed to the **Insolvency Practitioner**.

The temptation to get into debt is all around us. Just before we went to press, Rosy's dog Gussie received a letter inviting 'Ms Gussie Rabson' to take out a credit card. How she got on the mailing list is a mystery!

'It's not the end of the world' is a very glib thing to say, especially to someone whose home is at risk because they guaranteed a debt. But there is life after insolvency. In fiction, something did finally turn up for Mr Micawber, and young Tom Tulliver paid his father's business debts in full. In real life, too, there are bound to be people near you who have survived financial ruin and gone on to rebuild their lives.

Insolvency can happen to anyone, rich and successful or poor and struggling, feckless and extravagant or just plain unlucky. In the US a businessman is generally seen as not having tried very hard if he does not have a couple of insolvencies behind him. We can't all get it right first time – the important thing is to be honest and not let the situation drag on. Maybe you won't want another go, or maybe you can learn from your mistakes and become successful next time round.

Forms and documents

Statutory demand (Form 4.1)

Rule 4.5

Statutory Demand under section 123(1)(a) or 222(1)(a) of the Insolvency Act 1986

Warning

- This is an **important** document. This demand must be dealt with **within 21 days** after its service upon the company or a winding-up order could be made in respect of the company.

- Please read the demand and notes carefully.

Notes for Creditor	DEMAND

Notes for Creditor

- If the Creditor is entitled to the debt by way of assignment, details of the original creditor and any intermediary assignees should be given in part B on page 3.

- If the amount of debt includes interest not previously notified to the company as included in its liability, details should be given, including the grounds upon which interest is charged. The amount of interest must be shown separately.

- Any other charge accruing due from time to time may be claimed. The amount or rate of the charge must be identified and the grounds on which it is claimed must be stated.

- In either case the amount claimed must be limited to that which will have accrued due at the date of the demand.

- If signatory of the demand is a solicitor or other agent of the creditor the name of his/her firm should be given

DEMAND

To

Address

This demand is served on you by the creditor:

Name

Address

The creditor claims that the company will owe the sum of £ full particulars of which are set out on page 2.

The creditor demands that the company do pay the above debt or secure or compound for it to the creditor's satisfaction.

Signature of individual

Name
(BLOCK LETTERS)

Date

*Position with or relationship to creditor

*Delete if signed by the creditor himself.

*I am authorised to make this demand on the creditor's behalf

Address

Tel No   Ref.

N.B. The person making this demand must complete the whole of this page, page 2 and parts A and B (as applicable) on page 3.

4.1 Statutory demand under section 123(1)(a) or 222(1)(a)of the Insolvency Act 1986 09/2003   © Crown copyright. Produced by infolaw

Particulars of Debt
(These particulars must include (a) when the debt was incurred, (b) the consideration for
the debt (or if is there is no consideration the way in which it arose) and (c) the amount
due as at the date of this demand).

Notes for Creditor
Please make sure that you
have read the notes on page 1
before completing this page.

Note:
If space is insufficient continue
on reverse of page 3 and
clearly indicate on this page
that you are doing so.

4.1 Statutory demand under section 123(1)(a) or 222(1)(a)of the Insolvency Act 1986 09/2003

© Crown copyright Produced by infolaw

Part A

The individual or individuals to whom any communication regarding this demand may be addressed is/are:

Name

Address

Telephone Number

Reference

Part B

For completion if the creditor is entitled to the debt by way of assignment

	Name	Date(s) of Assignment
Original creditor		
Assignees		

How to comply with a statutory demand

If the company wishes to avoid a winding-up petition being presented it must pay the debt shown on page 1, particulars of which are set out on page 2 of this notice, within the period of **21 days after** its service upon the company. Alternatively, the company can attempt to come to a settlement with the creditor. To do this the company should:

* inform the individual (or one of the individuals) named in part A above immediately that it is willing and able to offer security for the debt to the creditor's satisfaction; or

* inform the individual (or one of the individuals) named in part A immediately that it is willing and able to compound for the debt to the creditor's satisfaction.

If the company disputes the demand in whole or in part it should:

* contact the individual (or one of the individuals) named in part A immediately.

REMEMBER!   **The company has only 21 days after the date of service on it of this document before the creditor may present a winding-up petition.**

4.1 Statutory demand under section 123(1)(a) or 222(1)(a)of the Insolvency Act 1986 09/2003   © Crown copyright. Produced by infolaw

Winding up petition (Form 4.2)

Rule 4.7   Form 4.2

Winding-Up Petition

(Title)   **(Registered No.   )**

(a) Insert title of court   To (a)

(b) Insert full name(s)
and address(es) of
petitioner(s)   The petition of (b)

(c) Insert full name
and registered no. of
company subject to
petition   1. (c)

                      (hereinafter called "the company") was incorporated on

(d) Insert date of
incorporation   (d)

                      under the Companies Act 19

(e) Insert address of
registered office   2. The registered office of the company is at (e)

(f) Insert amount of
nominal capital and
how it is divided   3. The nominal capital of the company is (f) £
(g) Insert amount of divided into   shares of £   each. The amount of the capital paid up or credited
capital paid up or   as paid up is (g) £
credited as paid up

                      4. The principal objects for which the company was established are as follows:

                      and other objects stated in the memorandum of association of the company

(h) Set out the
grounds on which a   5. (h)
winding-up order is
sought

(j) Delete as   6. The company (j) is/is not an insurance undertaking; a credit institution; an investment
applicable   undertaking providing services involving the holding of funds or securities for third
                      parties; or a collective investment undertaking as referred to in Article 1.2 of the EC
                      Regulation.

(k) Insert name of   7. For the reasons stated in the affidavit of (k)   filed in support
person swearing   here of it is considered that the EC Regulation on insolvency proceedings (j) will/will not
affidavit   apply (j) and that these proceedings will be (l)_____ proceedings as
                      defined in Article 3 of the EC Regulation
(l) Insert whether
main, secondary or
territorial proceedings

                      8. In the circumstances it is just and equitable that the company should be wound up
                      The petitioner(s) therefore pray(s) as follows:-

                      (1) that (c)

                      may be wound up by the court under the provisions of the Insolvency Act 1986
                      or
                      (2) that such other order may be made as the court thinks fit

Note: It is intended to serve this petition on (m) [the company] [and]

Endorsement

This petition having been presented to the court
on _____ will be heard at (n) [Royal Courts of Justice, Strand, London, WC2A 2LL] [(n) _____ County Court
_____]

(n) Insert name and address of Court

(o) Insert name and address of District Registry

[(o) _____ District Registry
_____]

on:

Date_____

Time _____hours
(or as soon thereafter as the petition can be heard)

The solicitor to the petitioner is:-

Name_____

Address_____

_____

Telephone no_____

Reference_____

(j) [Whose London Agents are:-

Name_____

Address_____

_____

Telephone no. _____

Reference_____

MINUTES OF THE MEETING OF THE BOARD OF DIRECTORS OF

Insolvent Limited

Held at: The office

On: 2 January 200X

Present: Mr Director
Mr Director

In Attendance: Advising Accountant

The company's financial position was discussed and it was resolved that:

1 It having been proved to the satisfaction of the meeting that the company cannot by reason of its liabilities continue its business, it was advisable to wind up the company voluntarily.

2 Instructions be and are hereby given to The Insolvency Firm to assist the directors in convening the statutory meetings of members and creditors in accordance with the Insolvency Act 1986.

3 Be appointed to act as Chairman of the statutory meetings of members and creditors.

4 Instructions be and are hereby given to The Insolvency Firm to assist the directors in the preparation of the Statement of Affairs and the report on the company's trading history to be given to the creditors.

5 The company's bank account be frozen with the bank instructed to make no further payments. A new bank account to be opened in the name of the company into which all monies received by the company should be paid. This new account to be used to discharge liabilities in respect of fees, costs and expenses properly incurred and arising from the implementation of the foregoing

resolutions including payments to employees and suppliers with the balance in that account, if any, to be passed to the liquidator following his appointment.

6   Be appointed on behalf of the board to swear the statement of affairs and to authorise the report on the company's trading history to be given to the creditors.

7   The fee for preparing the Statement of Affairs and calling the meetings of members and creditors be agreed in the sum of £1,000 plus VAT to exclude disbursements.

8   The company shall incur no further credit as from the time of this meeting and that the company's employees be instructed accordingly.

9   The company's registered office be changed to The Insolvency Firm's address.

Signed   ....

Director

Dated   ....

First letter to creditors

To all known creditors

31 May 200X

Dear Sirs

Insolvent Limited (in creditors' voluntary liquidation)

1 Appointment of liquidator

I was appointed liquidator of the above company following meetings of members and creditors held on 20 January 200X. I attach for your information a summary of the director's sworn Statement of Affairs together with the other information made available at the creditors' meeting which sets out the company's financial position and the events leading up to the liquidation.

2 Overview

The director's Statement of Affairs, which is drawn up without making an allowance for the cost of the liquidation, shows that preferential creditors would be paid in full and there would be funds of £115,000 available for the unsecured creditors.

My own initial assessment broadly agrees with the director's estimates for asset realisations and the quantum of creditors and on the assumption that our administration of this case proves to be straightforward I estimate the costs of the liquidation, including legal and agents' fees, at £15,000. On this basis the anticipated return to creditors is that preferential creditors will be paid in full and the unsecured creditors will received a dividend of 70p in the pound.

3 Assets

3.1 Contracts
As detailed in the director's Statement of Affairs, the contracts which were estimated to realise £68,000 were reviewed by quantity surveyors, who I have now instructed to assist me in collecting these.

3.2 Minor works
These are completed minor works jobs which the director estimates will realise £1,000.

3.3 Retentions
Quantity surveyors have been instructed to recover the outstanding retentions which the director estimated to realise £3,000.

3.4 Fixtures and fittings
I have now instructed [agents] to remove the assets for sale by auction.

3.5 Cash at bank
The director's Statement of Affairs shows that £50,000 was held in the company's bank account. I have written to the bankers and have asked for the money to be forwarded to me to place in the liquidation account.

4 Liabilities and dividend prospects

As stated above, preferential creditors should be paid in full and there should be a surplus available for unsecured creditors. Accordingly, creditors are required to submit their claims to me if they have not already done so, and I enclose a proof of debt form. It is not possible at this stage to give an accurate indication as to the likely quantum or timing of any dividend as this will depend on the level of realisations, the amount of claims agreed and the costs of the liquidation. I will report to creditors when I envisage being in a position to pay a dividend or otherwise annually.

5 Liquidation committee and liquidator's remuneration

No liquidation committee was appointed but the following resolutions were passed at the meeting:

- That the costs in respect of the section 98 creditors meeting of £   plus disbursements plus VAT be approved. This is to be drawn from asset realisations.
- That the remuneration of the liquidator be fixed on the basis of time properly spent by the liquidator and his staff in attending to matters arising in the liquidation and details of the actual hours spent and amount of remuneration drawn in accordance with the resolution will be disclosed in subsequent reports.

A creditor's guide to liquidator's fees is also attached.

6   Directors' conduct

As liquidator I have a duty to investigate the company's affairs and report on the conduct of the directors or any shadow directors. I would be pleased to receive any information which may assist in this investigation and enclose a questionnaire for completion.

Yours faithfully

Liquidator

Enclosures

Questionnaire on Director's Conduct
Insolvent Limited

I am required to carry out a preliminary investigation of the company and its directors. Your assistance by commenting on your trading relationship will help in this investigation.

1   Creditor's name and address.

2   Estimated gross claim.   £

3   Age of debt at date of liquidation:
      i   0–30 days   £
      ii   30–60 days   £
      iii   60–90 days   £
      iv   90–120 days   £
      v   over 120 days   £

4   What were your credit terms?

5   What was the average credit taken by the company?

6   What was the authorised credit limit?   £

7   If exceeded, on what basis was this allowed?

8   Please provide details of any comfort, security or assurance given to you to allow continuance of credit.

9   On approximately what date were you first aware that there were difficulties in obtaining payment?

10   What evidence do you have of this?

11   Did you take action against the company for recovery of your
      debt – please provide details.

12   Please provide details of any on account payments – first dates
      and amounts.

13   Please provide details of any cheques which were dishonoured –
      dates and amounts.

14   If there are other matters of which you feel I should be aware,
      please provide brief details.

Signature: ....

Date: ....

Position: ....

For and on behalf of: ....

PROOF OF DEBT – GENERAL FORM

**In the matter of Insolvent Limited
and in the matter of The Insolvency Act 1986**

1	Name of Creditor	
2	Address of Creditor	
3	Total amount of claim, including any Value Added Tax and outstanding uncapitalised interest as at the date the company went into liquidation	£
4	Details of any document by reference to which the debt can be substantiated [note the liquidator may call for any document or evidence to substantiate the claim at his discretion]	
5	If the total amount shown above includes Value Added Tax, please show: (a) amount of Value Added Tax (b) amount of claim NET of Value Added Tax	£ £
6	If total amount above includes outstanding uncapitalised interest, please state amount	£
7	If you have filled in both box 3 and box 5, please state whether you are claiming the amount shown in box 3 or the amount shown in box 5(b)	

CORPORATE INSOLVENCY

8	Give details of whether the whole or any part of the debt falls within any (and if so which) of the categories of preferential debts under section 386 of, and schedule 6 to, the Insolvency Act 1986 (as read with schedule 3 to the Social Security Pensions Act 1975)	Category Amount(s) claimed as preferential £
9	Particulars of how and when debt incurred	
10	Particulars of any security held, the value of the security, and the date it was given	£
11	Signature of creditor or person authorised to act on his behalf	
	Name in BLOCK LETTERS	
	Position with or relation to creditor	

Insolvent Limited

Report for the meeting of creditors called under section 98 of the Insolvency Act 1986 to be held at The Hotel on 20 January 2004

Statutory Information

You have on the attached schedule, details of incorporation, registered office, directors, shareholders and a summary of recent trading results.

Director's history of the business and reasons for failure

Insolvent Limited was incorporated on 6 February 199X to take over a previous business run as Building Partnership. The managing director, had been employed by the previous business for 19 years. The Company traded as installation engineers.

In the first year, turnover was £1,200,000 and the Company employed up to 13 operatives. By 2000 our contract value had increased and we were taking contracts of £350,000. In 2002 we took on one apprentice and a junior engineer. Our client base was considerable and consisted of Local Authority and other major corporates.

We are members of the normal governing bodies, ie, our health and safety policies were fully incorporated and we have never had any major accidents to report.

The Company had always traded profitably in the past. We were considering growing our turnover to £2 million plus in the next two years from carefully monitored and organised growth. To obtain this growth, meetings with our accountants took place and our bank was approached for the necessary funding. After exploring every avenue it was decided that we could not get enough financial backing at this time to go forward with this project but the Company continued to win contracts as before.

In December 199X a large contract for £340,000 was started, followed by a further large contract. Following delays in payments and contractual problems, cash flow problems occurred. In December 200X our accountants were called in to give an up to date balance sheet. This confirmed that the company had cash flow problems but on receipt of all outstanding contract balances was still very solvent and profitable. However, continued slow payments on some contracts meant we were unable to clear the cash flow, and further contractual problems led to the director to have further discussions with their accountants and contact business recovery and insolvency specialists for advice on November 200X. On their advice, speciality quantity surveyors were instructed to advise on the likely outcome of completed and partially completed contracts. Based on this advice the director decided to stop work on one contract which was likely to be loss making and collect the other outstanding contract debts.

As a result, the Company ceased to trade on 15 December 200X when most of the staff were made redundant. On a best estimate there would be more than sufficient funds to pay creditors in full. However, one large contractor continued to dispute the debt and the directors felt they should draw a line and place the Company into liquidation so that a liquidator could deal with the funds, further realisations and the creditors' claims.

The director regrets the need for this but in the end could not justify the risks of continued trading and believes this decision is best for all concerned. As shown by the attached statement there should be a substantial dividend to creditors.

Statement of Affairs

A summary of the director's Statement of Affairs for the company is attached together with a deficiency account.

Meeting of the company's members

A meeting of the members of Insolvent Limited was held earlier this morning at which the members resolved that the company should be voluntarily wound up and that the liquidator be appointed Liquidator of the Company.

My fee for assisting with the preparation of the Company's Statement of Affairs and convening the meeting of creditors pursuant to section 98 of the Insolvency Act 1986 is £   plus disbursements plus VAT which will be settled from asset realisations.

Formal resolutions

The formal business of the meeting will be as follows:

- The appointment of a liquidator by the creditors.

- The appointment of a liquidation committee if requested by creditors.
- The approval of the section 98 meeting costs.
- The approval of the basis of the liquidator's fees which are to be fixed on the basis of time properly spent by the liquidator and his staff in attending to matters arising in the liquidation. Details of actual hours spent and amount of remuneration drawn in accordance with the resolution will be disclosed in subsequent reports. A copy of 'a creditors' guide to liquidators' fees is attached.

Insolvent Limited
Company information

1	**Company number**	017345

2	**Date of incorporation**	6 February 199X

3 **Director's**

Name	Appointed	Resigned
MR Director	6 February 199X	Still in office

4 **Shareholders**

Name	Shares held
MR Director	1
MRS Director	1
	2

5 **Capital**

Authorised: 2 ordinary £1 shares
Issued and fully paid: 2 ordinary £1 shares

6 **Business** Installation

7 **Addresses**

Trading address:
The Workshop
The Industrial Estate
The Town

Registered office:
The Accountants
Office

8 **Accounts**

Period ended	Turnover	Gross profit	Directors' remuneration	Net profit after tax	Dividends	Balance on profit and loss a/c
	£000	£000	£000	£000	£000	£000
28/02/0X	840	121	29	27	nil	126
28/02/0X	890	173	30	70	nil	98
29/02/0X	880	90	28	12	nil	28

9 **Cause of Company's failure**
Loss making larger contracts.

Insolvent Limited
Director's estimated Statement of Affairs as at 2 May 200X

	Notes	Book value	Estimated to realise
		£000	£000
Assets not specifically pledged	1		
Contracts	1.1	84	68
Minor works	1.2	2	1
Retentions	1.3	8	3
Fixtures and Fittings	1.4	7	2
Cash at bank	1.5	50	50
Estimated total assets available for preferential creditors		164	124
Preferential creditors	2		
Employees	2.1	9	
			(9)
Estimated surplus as regard preferential creditors			115
Non preferential creditors	3		
Trade creditors	3.1	93	
PAYE and VAT		12	
Employees	3.2	30	
			(135)
Estimated deficiency as regard creditors			(20)
Issued and called up share capital			Nil
Estimated total deficiency (subject to costs of winding up)			(20)

Insolvent Limited

Notes to the director's estimated Statement of Affairs

1   Assets not specifically pledged

1.1   The outstanding contracts have been reviewed by quantity surveyors who estimate that the remaining three contracts should realise £68,000.

1.2   These represent completed minor works jobs which the director estimates will realise £1,000.

1.3   These represent retentions which the director estimates will realise £3,000.

1.4   These assets have been independently valued by professional valuers, George Hazell & Co, and the amounts shown on the statement of affairs reflect the values on an *in situ* basis.

1.5   This represents £50,000 held in the Company's bank account.

2   Preferential creditors

2.1   This represents the last month's wages.

3   Non preferential creditors

3.1   A full list of creditors is attached.

3.2   This is the estimate of accrued redundancy and pay in lieu of notice entitlements arising following the closure of the business on the 24 March 200X.

Insolvent Limited

Estimated deficiency account for the period 1 March 200X to 2 May 200X

	£'000
Shareholders' funds at 1 March 200X	126

Amounts written off for the purpose		
of preparing the Statement of Affairs		
Contracts	16	
Minor works	1	
Retentions	5	
Fixtures and fittings	5	
		27
		99

	£'000
Estimated trading loss for the period	
1 March 200X to 2 May 200X	(119)
Estimated deficiency according to the	
Statement of Affairs	(20)

Lookingahead limited

Profit & Loss Account Forecast
Year Ending 31st December 200X

	January	February	March	April	May	June	July	August	September	October	November	December	Total
Sales	38,003	49,480	59,780	69,596	70,153	70,587	60,587	52,300	72,300	67,300	67,300	52,100	729,486
Cost of Sales	8,000	12,000	13,000	15,000	15,000	15,000	16,000	14,000	14,000	14,000	14,000	14,000	164,000
Direct Expenses	12,864	19,864	20,797	20,797	20,797	21,267	21,267	21,267	23,767	23,767	23,767	23,767	253,988
Gross Profit/(Loss)	17,139	17,616	25,983	33,799	34,356	34,320	23,320	17,033	34,533	29,533	29,533	14,333	311,498
	45.10%	35.60%	43.46%	48.56%	48.97%	48.62%	38.49%	32.57%	47.76%	43.88%	43.88%	27.51%	42.70%
Overheads	21,057	21,807	21,807	21,807	21,807	21,807	21,807	22,201	22,201	22,201	22,201	22,201	262,904
Trading Profit/(Loss)	(3,918)	(4,191)	4,176	11,992	12,549	12,513	1,513	(5,168)	12,332	7,332	7,332	(7,868)	48,594
Accum. Profit	(3,918)	(8,109)	(3,933)	8,059	20,608	33,121	34,634	29,466	41,798	49,130	56,462	48,594	

Cashflow Forecast
Year Ending 31st December 200X

	January	February	March	April	May	June	July	August	September	October	November	December	Total
Sales inc. VAT	44,654	58,139	70,242	81,775	82,430	82,940	71,190	61,453	84,953	79,078	79,078	61,218	857,146
Receipts from sales (inc. VAT)	50,830	66,372	65,849	68,783	73,928	78,495	74,895	68,795	84,248	76,317	72,909	69,525	850,944
Total Expenditure inc. VAT	41,921	55,371	60,004	60,204	60,204	60,674	61,674	60,068	62,568	62,568	62,568	62,568	710,392
VAT Payment	0	16,717	0	0	16,481			19,520			18,466		71,184
CVA Contribution/loan payments	2,000	2,000	2,000	2,000	2,000	2,000	2,000	3,000	3,000	4,000	4,000	4,000	32,000
Total Cash Outgoings	43,921	74,088	62,004	62,204	78,685	62,674	63,674	82,588	65,568	66,568	85,034	66,568	813,576
net inflow/(outflow)	6,909	(7,716)	3,845	6,579	(4,757)	15,821	11,221	(13,793)	18,680	9,749	(12,125)	2,957	37,368
Opening Balance	7,852	14,761	7,045	10,890	17,468	12,711	28,533	39,753	25,960	44,640	54,389	42,264	45,220
Closing Balance	14,761	7,045	10,890	17,468	12,711	28,533	39,753	25,960	44,640	54,389	42,264	45,220	45,220

Notes to cash flow forecasts

The forecast on the previous page is in a summary form and you may need more details of the expenses and receipts or alternatively have a supporting schedule which backs up the figures on the summary. When preparing the forecast it is essential to have a list of assumptions and notes as to how you have calculated the various figures and these would include the following.

Sales

In the profit forecast everything is done net of VAT and you will see that in the cash flow forecast the corresponding figure includes VAT. In this case the money from sales is received in the same month as the sale. However, in many cases the receipt may not be received for a month or two and this will need to be reflected in the cash flow. So you need to put the January sales into the cash flow forecast as being received two months later, say in March.

Cost of sales

Cost of sales here would be purchases required to make those sales and direct expenses which are normally expenses directly relating to the cost of producing the sales and vary in proportion to the sale. You need to take account of when you are going to have to pay these so wages on a shop floor may be paid immediately and goods may be paid one month later and that should be reflected in the cash flow statement.

Gross profit

It is always good to show the gross profit and the profit percentage to see whether the above figures make sense and are in line with your expectations.

Overheads

We have only shown one figure for overheads but you may wish to have a supporting schedule with greater detail of rent, overheads, wages, motor expenses, etc.

These may not vary directly in line with sales and many will be fixed costs. With the cash flow statement you need to put these down when they are paid; for example, rent may be paid quarterly and we show VAT separately because it is often a large figure.

Cash flow statement

The cash flow statement is designed to show when you actually paid for something and is done in gross of VAT. In this example we have shown the contribution that may be made in a company voluntary arrangement or this could be loan repayments to a bank, for example.

Closing balance

The closing balance on the cash flow statement shows the balance at the bank at the end of each month. In this example the balance is quite similar to the profit because there are no unusual items and because of factoring it is like a cash business. In this particular instance VAT has quite a big effect. You may have capital expenditure at odd times or rent payments which will throw the cash balance out from the profit.

Total

It is always vital to have a total figure and ideally this should be reconciled with an opening and closing balance sheet.

Useful contacts

Department of Trade and Industry (DTI)

www.dti.gov.uk

There is much free information on this site, which also links with, among others, Companies House and the Insolvency Service. It also provides the Enterprise Act 2002 and a user's guide to the Act – go to the list of topics and select 'Enterprise Act'.

The Insolvency Service Public Enquiry Line

Tel: 020 7291 6895

Email: central.enquiryline@insolvency.gsi.gov.uk

The Insolvency Service website

For obtaining leaflets online: www.insolvency.gov.uk

The Insolvency Service is a section of the DTI and its useful website contains details of all the various receivers and government bodies dealing with insolvency. The home page provides links to useful articles on all aspects of individual and corporate insolvency, as well as links with many professional bodies, some of which we also review below.

Publications Order Line

For copies of useful leaflets, especially the *Guide to Bankruptcy*:

Tel: 0121 698 4241

Or write to:

The Insolvency Service
(Publications Orders)
Records Management
4th Floor East
Ladywood House
Birmingham B2 4UZ

HM Customs and Excise (VAT)

Just to prove that the VAT man has a heart after all, HMCE offers a website called National Insolvency Unit on www.hmce.gov.uk. It offers free guidance leaflets as well as a telephone helpdesk, manned 8.30 am – 5 pm Monday to Thursday and 8.30 am – 4 pm Friday.

Insolvency Helpdesk: 0151 703 8450

Fax: 0151 703 8735

Email: go to the website and click on 'Insolvency Helpdesk'.

Professional bodies

Many professional bodies' websites are linked to the Insolvency Service website. Here's a selection:

Association of Business Recovery Professionals (R3 online)

www.r3.org.uk (short for Rescue, Recovery, Renewal).

Most Insolvency Practitioners are members of their own trade organisation, the Association of Business Recovery Professionals. This website gives basic insolvency information and details of how to make a complaint.

Insolvency Practitioners' Association

www.ipa.uk.com

Here you'll find useful free information as well as links to several related sites.

Many Insolvency Practitioners have their own websites with detailed information on different types of insolvency. Search under Insolvency Practitioner.

Companies House

www.companieshouse.gov.uk

Your first port of call for corporate insolvency. The website offers guidance leaflets on liquidation, CVAs, etc.

Insolvency statistics

If you want to find out about insolvency statistics – eg, how many liquidations there are, or who is handling which liquidation – this can generally be found on www.insolvency.co.uk. This site has a list of Insolvency Practitioners, as does the Government Insolvency Service website (see above).

Checking creditworthiness

The Register of County Court Judgments

The Register is maintained by

Registry Trust Limited
173–175 Cleveland Street
London W1T 6QR
Tel: 020 7380 0133

www.registry-trust.org.uk

For £4.50 per name (make out the cheque to Registry Trust Limited) you can get a print-out of any judgments against that name.

Business Debt Line

Tel: 0800 197 6026 Monday – Friday 10 am – 4 pm, plus 24-hour answering machine service.

www.bdl.org.uk

Free telephone debt counselling for the self-employed and small business facing insolvency. Advice is free, independent and confidential.

Community Legal Service

Run by the Legal Services Commission, formerly the Legal Aid Board. Solicitors who participate in its scheme can give free legal advice if you qualify.

Tel: 0845 608 1122 for a solicitor near you.

Or access their website: www.justask.org.uk

Small Business Service Single Gateway

This government agency helps small businesses and provides them with high quality information.

Tel: 0845 600 9006

www.businesslink.gov.uk

Citizens Advice Bureaux

The National Association of Citizens Advice Bureaux website offers general advice on debt as well as details of CAB offices near you. Or check your local telephone directory for a CAB near you.

www.nacab.org.uk

Redundancy Payments Office

The Insolvency Service Redundancy Payments Office has a helpline to deal with employees' concerns following the insolvency of their employer and the progress of their claims.

Tel: 0500 848 489

Advertising (missing shareholders, details of winding up, etc)

The London Gazette
PO Box 7923
London SW8 5WF

Tel: 020 7394 4580

You can advertise online at www.gazettes-online.co.uk or over the telephone: 020 7873 8308 (direct line to their Advertising Manager) using your credit card.

The cost of a single insertion is £36.80 (inclusive of VAT) – cheques are payable to the *London Gazette*.

Give at least two days' notice of the date you wish the advertisement to appear.

Index

Notes

Notes

Notes

Notes

The *Pocket Lawyer* series

Corporate Insolvency	Andrew McTear, Chris Williams, Frank Brumby & Rosy Border
Debt Recovery	Mark Fairweather & Rosy Border
Divorce and Separation	Rosy Border & Jane Moir
Letting Your Property	Rosy Border & Mark Fairweather
Living Wills and Enduring Powers of Attorney	Mark Fairweather & Rosy Border
Personal Insolvency	Andrew McTear, Chris Williams, Frank Brumby & Rosy Border
Setting Up a Limited Company	Mark Fairweather & Rosy Border
Taking in a Lodger	Rosy Border
The Employer's Handbook	Bob Watt & Rosy Border
Wills and Estate Planning	Mark Fairweather & Rosy Border
Your Consumer Rights	Angela Clark & Rosy Border
Your Rights at Work	Bob Watt & Rosy Border

To order any of the titles in the *Pocket Lawyer* series, contact

Cavendish Publishing Limited
The Glass House
Wharton Street
London WC1X 9PX
email: info@cavendishpublishing.com
web: www.cavendishpublishing.com
Tel: 020 7278 8000
Fax: 020 7278 8080